ROUSSEAU:
A GUIDE FOR THE PERPLEXED

Guides for the Perplexed available from Continuum:

ROUSSEAU: A GUIDE FOR THE PERPLEXED

MATTHEW SIMPSON

continuum

Continuum International Publishing Group
The Tower Building   80 Maiden Lane
11 York Road   Suite 704
London SE1 7NX   New York
                                      NY 10038

British Library Cataloguing-in-Publication Data
A catalogue record for this book is available from the British Library.

ISBN HB: 0-8264-8939-7   9780826489395
ISBN PB: 0-8264-8940-0   9780826489401

Library of Congress Cataloging-in-Publication Data
Simpson, Matthew.
Rousseau : a guide for the perplexed / Matthew Simpson.
        p.   cm. – (Guides for the perplexed)
Includes bibliographical references and index.
ISBN-13: 978-0-8264-8939-5
ISBN-10: 0-8264-8939-7
ISBN-13: 978-0-8264-8940-1
1. Rousseau, Jean-Jacques, 1712–1778. I. Title. II. Series.
B2137.S56   2007
194—dc22

                                              2006028508

Typeset by Servis Filmsetting Ltd, Manchester
Printed and bound in
Great Britain by Cromwell Press Ltd,
Trowbridge, Wiltshire

To Regan

CONTENTS

ABBREVIATIONS

J = Maurice Cranston, *Jean-Jacques: The Early Life and Work of Jean-Jacques Rousseau, 1712–1754* (Chicago: University of Chicago Press, 1991).

N = Maurice Cranston, *The Noble Savage: Jean-Jacques Rousseau, 1754–1762* (Chicago: University of Chicago Press, 1991).

D = Jean-Jacques Rousseau, *The Discourses and Other Early Political Writings*, ed. and trans. Victor Gourevitch (Cambridge: Cambridge University Press, 1997).

S = Jean-Jacques Rousseau, *The Social Contract and Other Later Political Writings*, ed. and trans. Victor Gourevitch (Cambridge: Cambridge University Press, 1997).

E = Jean-Jacques Rousseau, *Emile: Or on Education*, trans. Allan Bloom (New York: Basic Books, 1979).

C = Jean-Jacques Rousseau, *Confessions*, trans. J. M. Cohen (London: Penguin Books, 1953).

PREFACE

This book is intended to introduce readers to the philosophical writings of Jean-Jacques Rousseau. Because his genius expressed itself in many genres, including plays, operas, novels, poems, speeches, treatises and scientific textbooks, it was difficult to decide what to include in this short volume. Rousseau himself provided some guidance, however. In a famous letter of 1762, when he was at the end of the most creative period of his life and suffering from debilitating illness, he paused to evaluate his philosophical accomplishments. From his large body of work he selected three texts as his 'principal writings', namely his 'Discourse on the Sciences and Arts', his 'Discourse on the Origin and Foundations of Inequality' and his philosophical novel *Emile*. It is a measure of his good judgement, and ours, that these works have also been among the most influential on later generations. In addition, I have included a chapter on his political treatise *The Social Contract* because, although he professed to have a low opinion of this work, many philosophers consider it a masterpiece and, in any case, it has been among the most studied of all his writings, never more so than today.

Within this selection of his work I have focused on the ideas and arguments that have been of enduring philosophical interest and especially those that are likely to confuse readers who are approaching his writings for the first time. My goal has been to provide background information that will help the reader through many of the apparent paradoxes in his works and, when his meaning still remains obscure, to clarify the nature of the problem. In the most difficult interpretative controversies, I have striven to give tools for further reflection and research rather than simply stating my opinion. I hope that the reader will find this to be stimulating rather than merely inconclusive.

I would like to thank Luther College for its considerable financial support. I also benefited greatly from Christopher Kelly's unparalleled knowledge of Rousseau's life and works. This book is dedicated to my wife Regan, without whose advice, criticism and support it would have been impossible to complete.

CHAPTER 1

HIS LIFE AND WORKS

.

Jean-Jacques Rousseau was an unusual man. He was a shy artist who admired generals and conquerors. He valued friendship above all things and yet died alone. He wrote a masterpiece on education while abandoning his own children to orphanages. He extolled civic virtue while being chased from three different countries. He contributed to the greatest scientific enterprise of his age yet believed that science corrupts morality. He composed a successful lyric opera in French while arguing that the French language is unsuited to lyricism. Almost alone among his philosophical peers he believed in the immortality of the soul and personal salvation yet his books were burned throughout Europe for their impiety. He wrote the best-selling novel of his century while decrying literature, and then went on to marry a woman who (it is said) could not even read. He was simultaneously bashful and aggressive, an ascetic and a voluptuary, a citizen and a recluse. Few would question his claim that, 'I am made unlike anyone I have ever met; I will even venture to say that I am like no one in the whole world. I may be no better, but at least I am different' (C 17).

Yet, from his volatile character and the chaos of his personal life emerged many of the acknowledged masterpieces of the eighteenth century. These books have carried his name to every country on earth and their ideas have affected almost everyone alive in one way or another. Luckily, a remarkable record survives of this remarkable man. Scholars have collected over 50 volumes of his letters along with all of his published writing and much of his unpublished work. There is also vast documentary evidence of his life, travels, friendships and quarrels. Above all, however, he wrote a series of autobiographical works, most notably his *Confessions*, which are classics of world literature and provide a kind of insight into his life and character that has few parallels in the history of philosophy. His life unfolded in three parts. His youth, filled with wandering, struggle and intermittent education, ended when, at the age of 30, he moved to Paris, the cultural centre of Europe. He spent the second part of his life in and around the French capital, where he experienced a series of artistic and literary triumphs that made him one of the most famous and influential men of his time. This period ended when, at 50, he became the victim of political persecution and, some have suggested, growing madness. During the last part of his life, between escaping France at 50 and his death at 66, he suffered from increasing unhappiness and paranoia. Yet even during his last years he produced some of his most striking and enduring work. His life was rich in every conceivable dimension, so the following survey will focus on the people and events that were most important for his philosophical development.

1. YOUTH (1712–1742)

Jean-Jacques Rousseau was born in Geneva on 28 June, 1712, the son of Susan and Isaac Rousseau. Although his mother was descended from one of the city's most prominent families, his birth was an unhappy occasion. She was 39 years old and died a few days after the delivery. His father was a watchmaker and a member of Geneva's class of highly skilled artisans. Yet he was not the social equal of his wife and, after her death, financial necessity forced him to move from their fashionable townhouse to a modest home in a workers' neighbourhood, where Rousseau spent the first ten years of his life. The father seemed to blame his son for the decline in their fortune and found ways to get revenge by occasionally beating him and spending the money left to him by his mother. Yet Rousseau's boyhood was generally happy and did much to fix the course of his adult life.

He learned to read while very young and his schooling, such as it was, came from reading to himself and to his father while the latter worked at his watchmaker's bench. The first books given to him, at the age of four or five, were popular French romance novels from the previous century by authors such as De Scudéry and La Calprenède. These books, with their dashing heroes, fair maidens and subtle analysis of human emotion, had a profound influence on the young Rousseau. He later wrote, 'In a short time I acquired by this dangerous method, not only an extreme facility in reading and expressing myself, but a singular insight for my age into the passions. I had no idea of the facts, but I was already familiar with every feeling. I had grasped nothing; I had sensed everything' (C 20).

By the time he was seven, however, he advanced to a different kind of reading, with a different effect on his outlook. From his mother's family he had inherited a small library of Greek, Latin and French classics. So, for the next three years he immersed himself in these works, which included the writings of Ovid, Bossuet, Fontenelle, Molière and others. Of the ancient authors, one in particular had the greatest influence on him. 'Plutarch, of them all', he wrote, 'was my especial favorite, and the pleasure I took in reading and re-reading him did something to cure me of my passion for novels' (C 20). The image of civic virtue that he found in Plutarch's *Lives* forever shaped his view of human life. 'Continuously preoccupied with Rome and Athens, living as one might say with their great men, myself born the citizen of a republic and the son of a father whose patriotism was his strongest passion, I took fire by his example and pictured myself as a Greek or a Roman' (C 20).

When he was ten, however, his life suddenly changed. One day his father struck a French army officer with his sword after a real or perceived insult. Believing correctly that he would find himself in trouble with the legal authorities, Isaac fled to a town outside the jurisdiction of Geneva's courts. Indeed, he spent the remainder of his life in exile, giving up his trade as a watchmaker, remarrying and living on the income of his first wife's estate. Rather than accompanying his father into this ignominious retirement, however, Rousseau was put in the care of a wealthy uncle on his mother's side who had a son his own age. The two cousins became close friends and were sent to school in the home of a local pastor where Rousseau gained nearly the only formal education he would ever have.

The pastor lived in a village just beyond the walls of Geneva and, in this rural setting, Rousseau had a further series of experiences that did much to shape his thought and set the trajectory of his later life. Some of them deepened and reinforced the dispositions he had acquired in Geneva, especially his sense of martial virtue and love of justice. For example, one day he was accused of breaking a household item, to which he earnestly pleaded his innocence. He was beaten for it, and then beaten more severely when the first round of abuse failed to draw a confession from him. He later said that he was never the same after this first meeting with violent injustice. 'The feeling was only a personal one in its origins, but it has since assumed such a consistency and has become so divorced from personal interests, that my blood boils at the sight or tale of any injustice, whoever may be the sufferer and wherever it may have taken place' (C 30). Yet his time in the country also softened his sense of civic virtue and reawakened in him some of the feelings from his early reading of romance novels. In particular, his friendship with his cousin had a lasting influence on his sense of human relations, for it provided a model of sincerity, mutual affection and enjoyment of common pursuits that stayed with him as an ideal for a certain kind of bond.

Perhaps the most important effect of this country life, however, had nothing to do either with his cousin or with his formal education. Rather, the alpine surroundings themselves kindled in him the love of nature that became such a famous and influential part of his character. He later said of this time, 'The country too was such a fresh experience that I could never have enough of it. Indeed the taste that I got for it was so strong that it has remained inextinguishable, and the memory of the happy days I spent there has made me long regretfully for a country life and its pleasures at every stage of my existence' (C 23–4). One can see in all of these occasions the beginning of his unique philosophical perspective. Of course, we know about these early incidents only because of what he wrote about them as an adult, so they are already shaped by his mature outlook. Yet they indicate the dominant themes of his philosophical writings: the importance of spontaneous friendship, the value of patriotic self-sacrifice, the virtues of rural life, respect for manual labour and hatred of injustice and arbitrary power.

His rural sojourn did not last, however. While modern scholars debate exactly how long he stayed with the pastor, it is certain that his formal education ended by the time he was 13. His uncle made it clear to him that he was of a lower social rank than his cousin, so when the latter went on to more advanced studies Rousseau was left behind to make his own way. His uncle would no longer support him, and his own father was content to leave him to fend for himself. In the end he was apprenticed to an engraver, whom he soon discovered to be an especially cruel and ignorant man. The months that followed were the saddest of Rousseau's boyhood, during which he acquired not only the basics of the engraver's art but also the vices of his surroundings. He later wrote of the time, 'My master's tyranny finally made a trade which I should have liked quite unbearable to me, and drove me to vices I should otherwise have despised, such as falsehood, idleness, and theft' (C 40). These miseries lead him to the most significant decision of his life.

On a Sunday evening when he was 15, Rousseau returned late from a walk in the countryside to find that the city gates had already been locked. It had happened to him twice before, so he knew the beatings and other punishments that awaited him at the hands of his master the next morning. Reflecting on the causes of his unhappiness, he made the fateful decision to run away from home. With no money, no skills, no connections, no possessions and no education, he simply turned around and walked out of Geneva and into the wider world. This decision marked the middle point of his youth. During the next 15 years he hardly set foot in his home city again, but instead experienced a remarkable series of adventures and mishaps.

To appreciate the course of Rousseau's life during the following years, one must understand something about the political situation of his native city. Geneva at the time was not part of the nation of Switzerland but was rather an independent Calvinist city-state. It was also virtually surrounded by Catholic enemies. One result was that the countryside around Geneva provided extraordinary opportunities for an articulate young Protestant willing to be flexible with his religious convictions. This was Rousseau's only advantage, and he used it. He turned south into the Catholic territory of Savoy where he met priests who were eager to offer shelter and support to a bright young man whom they might have the honour of converting to their faith. Eventually he was sent to the home of a young Catholic convert who earned a pension from the King of Sardinia for giving help to Protestants willing to change their religion. The young woman was Françoise-Louise de la Tour, Baroness de Warens. She was 29 years old, and would come to have more influence on Rousseau than perhaps any other person in his life.

First she arranged for him to journey to Turin, the capital of the province, where he could abjure his Calvinist faith and also find a way to support himself. He did as instructed and formally converted on 21 April, 1728. Much has been written about the meaning of Rousseau's conversion to Catholicism, yet at the time the decision was practical rather than spiritual. He needed help and this was the best way to get it. As an adult he had little regard for organized religion of any kind, Catholic or Protestant, and eventually both groups persecuted him severely. Even as a merely practical step, however, his boyhood conversion did not serve its purpose. Although the priests in Turin solicited funds to help him start a new life, the collection was very small, and he was left much as he began. He later wrote, 'Thus all my grand hopes were eclipsed in one moment, and all that had accrued from the self-interested step I had just taken was the memory of having become simultaneously an apostate and a dupe' (C 74).

So, he began to look for work in Turin. One can imagine that as a teenager with no connections and few marketable skills he had a hard time. Unable to support himself doing odd jobs, he finally accepted employment as a liveried footman in the household of a wealthy family. This was a very low station in the social hierarchy of the age, and he felt degraded by it. Wearing a servant's uniform and waiting on others caused him great embarrassment and the memory of it pained him in later life. Eventually he changed employers and, although he continued to work as a footman, the new family included a highly educated son who was preparing for leadership in the Church. Rousseau worked for him as a kind of personal secretary and in that way he learned Italian and had opportunities to demonstrate his natural intelligence. In fact, he quickly became a favourite.

His new employer began tutoring him in Latin and Italian literature and gradually rekindled in him the love of learning that had been extinguished by his life as an engraver's apprentice and a servant. Eventually the family suggested to him that, with their patronage, he might rise to a higher social status and obtain employment that would offer greater scope to his talents, such as in diplomacy or the civil service. Although he was pleased by their support, he was continually pained by his life as a servant, a pain that was aggravated by his belief that somehow the life into which he had fallen was unworthy of him. Thus, just as his future began to look more promising, he abandoned his employers without warning or apology. He left Turin with a charming vagabond whom he had met on the streets of the city.

With no other prospects he now returned across the Alps and presented himself unannounced at Mme de Warens' house, literally throwing himself at her feet. She took him in and agreed to help him find his way in the world. First she sent him to a local seminary to train as a priest, but he quickly dropped out because of a supposed inability to learn Latin, even though he had learned Italian very quickly in Turin. Next, he took up music, for which he had a great talent, in the hope of earning his way as a music teacher. Yet, although he was an amazingly quick student, his talents were not yet great enough to support him. Finally, Mme de Warens found employment for him in the civil service, working as a surveyor in a tax office. He laboured at this respectable and promising job for a few months, but he disliked it and soon quit. Once again, his inability to endure temporary hardship for future success ruined a promising career.

Yet, in the end, his failure to stay employed led to a welcome solution; indeed it led to perhaps the happiest period of his life. Having tried in vain to find a job for him, Mme de Warens now simply invited him to stay with her indefinitely. He agreed, and for most of the next decade he lived with her in Savoy, first merely as her boarder and later as her secretary and lover. These years between quitting the tax office in 1732 and moving to Paris in 1742 were generally a period of tranquillity and satisfaction that was most welcome after his wanderings. It was also a period of intense self-education, during which, with Mme de Warens' help, he came into his mature powers as a musical composer and began cultivating his philosophical and literary talents.

Although he had no formal teachers, he had an extraordinary desire for knowledge and did the best he could on his own. Mme de Warens had little time for lessons, but she helped him by means of her casual conversation, as did an educated gentleman who lived in their neighbourhood, of whom Rousseau later wrote, 'The seeds of literature and philosophy, which were beginning to stir in my brain, and which required only a little care and competition émulation for their complete development, found both in him' (C 205). In particular they discussed Voltaire, whose works deeply impressed Rousseau. He said, 'Nothing Voltaire wrote escaped us. The pleasures I derived from these readings fired me with the desire of learning to write a good style, and for trying to imitate the fine effects of this writer who so delighted me.' And it was not only the style of Voltaire's work that impressed him but the substance as well. 'A little later his *Philosophical Letters* appeared and, although they are certainly not his best work, it was they that most attracted me toward learning, my taste for which was born at that time and has never been extinguished since' (C 205).

Although he studied haphazardly, he tried to plan a course of education based on popular textbooks of the time. By any measurement he was a precocious and gifted student. For example, in a letter to a bookseller that survives from the period he ordered, among other works, Bayle's *Historical and Critical Dictionary* and the complete works of Cicero. The portion of his *Confessions* dealing with this time shows him not only reading Descartes, Malebranche, Locke and Leibniz but also teaching himself geometry, astronomy, geography, history and musical theory. He also began to compose music and poetry. His first publication was a song called 'The Merry Butterfly', which appeared in 1737, and shortly afterwards he published a poem entitled, 'The Orchard of Baroness de Warens'.

The poem is valuable in part because of the insight it offers into this period of Rousseau's self-education. It depicts him relaxing in Mme de Warens' garden and it mentions many books that he was reading at the time. Some of them seem appropriate to the bucolic setting, including the works of popular English and French literary authors such as Montaigne, Racine and Pope. But, interestingly, the majority of the authors he mentions are scientists and philosophers, including Plato, Kepler and Newton. It is hard to imagine that a young man sitting alone in an orchard in a Catholic backwater could have taught himself the ideas of some of the most sophisticated thinkers of all time. Yet apparently it happened. It is true that Mme de Warens hosted a modest salon where Rousseau heard scientific and theological discussions; yet his progress was nonetheless remarkable. If the poem is close to an honest summary of his time in Savoy, its shows that by his mid-twenties he had taught himself to understand the leading authors of modern science and philosophy.

Yet there was a less pleasant side to this period of his life. His health had never been strong and during the 1730s he suffered a major physical collapse. His description of its onset is still painful to read. 'One morning, on which I was no more ill than usual, I was putting a little table upon its legs when I felt a sudden almost inconceivable disturbance throughout my whole body. I cannot describe it better than as a kind of storm which started in my blood and instantly took control of my limbs' (C 217). He was bedridden for weeks and never really recovered. The remainder of his life was spent in some degree of physical suffering, which included insomnia, fatigue, dizziness and ringing in the ears. Because he left many descriptions of his ailment, later scholars have been able to diagnose his condition in light of more advanced medical science than existed in his time. The consensus is that he suffered from a chronic infection of his urinary tract, which was mostly untreatable at the time. In any case, all of the dozens of treatments he tried were extremely painful and complete failures, so by middle age he swore off doctors forever.

In the early stages of the illness Rousseau was convinced that he was dying, which made him think more seriously about his mortality than he had in the past. Coincidentally, his programme of study had led him at the same time to read the great philosophers of seventeenth-century France including Arnauld, Pascal and other thinkers associated with the religious community located at Port-Royal. The members of this community were famous for their defence and elaboration of the views of Cornelius Jansen, a Catholic bishop who emphasized the doctrine of original sin and the inability of a person to achieve salvation without divine grace. Jansen in turn had been inspired by the writings of St Augustine, who had argued for the view that, after the Fall, every human soul is corrupt and incapable of earning salvation on its own merits. One can imagine that this reading was not very comforting.

Rousseau later wrote of his outlook during this period, 'The writings of Port-Royal and the Oratory being my most frequent reading, had made me half a Jansenist, and sometimes, for all my trust in God, I was really frightened by their harsh theology. The fear of Hell, which had bothered me very little before, gradually disturbed my ease of mind' (C 230). In fact, subsequent research has uncovered a prayer written by Rousseau at this time that reveals much about his religious outlook. 'My conscience tells me, O Lord, how much I am guilty. I see that all the pleasures which my passions have prompted me to seek, at the expense of wisdom, have been worse than illusory, and are turned into odious bitterness' (J 135). St Augustine himself might have written these lines and of course it is not a coincidence that Rousseau called one of his greatest works *Confessions*, after a similar word by St Augustine.

Yet he survived this illness and eventually felt that his time with Mme de Warens should end. She had encountered financial difficulty that made it impossible to support him any longer and he, for his part, became resentful and jealous when she took in a second young man as an assistant. His letters and autobiography also suggest that by this time he had formed aspirations to enter the wider world of music and letters, which was virtually impossible from his isolated location in Savoy. So he began by accepting a job as tutor in Lyon to the sons of a local nobleman. The household was full of highly educated and influential people who formed a kind of micro-cosm of all the trends in contemporary high culture. As one scholar has said, 'The young man who had just resolved to dedicate the rest of his days to God found himself among the leading votaries of Reason' (J 142).

His employer had two younger brothers who, like Rousseau, would go on to become very distinguished in the world of literature and ideas. They were still young and unknown when Rousseau went to work for their elder brother, yet they soon befriended him and began to influence him in ways that are hard to measure. Radical and articulate, they were his first encounter with the full force of the French Enlightenment. One of the brothers was the Abbé de Mably, an early social scientist, while the other was the Abbé de Condillac, who was then only in his mid-twenties and not yet famous for his radical defence of John Locke's theory that the human mind is a 'blank slate'. Condillac was the first of the great eighteenth-century philosophers whom Rousseau met and he greatly benefited by this connection when he finally moved to Paris. The second reason this period is important is that, as a tutor, he first began to frame his ideas about education. In truth he failed badly as a teacher, yet he gained experience that he would draw on for the remainder of his life. When his contract was not renewed after the first year he returned to Mme de Warens, but he now found her house to be depressing and suffocating, and they still had no money. So, he decided to make the decisive step and move to Paris. In the spring of 1742 he left Mme de Warens' house for the last time.

2. ASCENDANCY (1742–1762)

In some ways, Rousseau's prospects must have seemed very dim. Paris had as large a concentration of youthful talent and ambition as any city in the world, making it very hard for a newcomer to be noticed. Moreover he was poor, a foreigner and nearly friendless. Yet he had a few advantages and he used them to great effect. First, he carried letters of introduction from the Mably family and their friends in Lyon, which gave him entry into the highest social circles of the metropolis. More important, however, he had his talent and ambition. While most 30-year-olds have completed their education, Rousseau was in a sense just beginning his. The powers of self-education that he exercised during the preceding decade would only grow during the two that followed. And the capacities for musical and literary composition that he developed in Turin and Savoy were just barely coming into maturity as he reached Paris. Also counting in his favour were the artistic and scientific works that he had already completed and now hoped to introduce in Paris. He brought with him a proposal for a new system of musical notation, as well as a draft of a comic play called 'Narcissus, or the Lover of Himself' and a collection of poems.

Almost immediately upon his arrival he was invited to present his 'Project for a New Musical Notation' to the Academy of Sciences. Unfortunately for him, a number of competent members of the Academy immediately found problems in the system, which were confirmed by the greatest French composer and musical theorist of the age, Jean-Philippe Rameau. In the end the Academy declined to endorse it. Yet the presentation earned the respect of important people and he quickly ingratiated himself with Parisian high society. Furthermore, the presentation helped him further refine his ideas on music. Soon after arriving in Paris he wrote his 'Dissertation on Modern Music', which was issued the following year and was his first major prose publication. This was quickly followed by the successful publication of a poem he had written in Lyon, 'Letter to Monsieur Bordes', and during the following months he continued to work on 'Narcissus' and began work on a new French-style opera, *The Gallant Muses*.

Although he met friendship, encouragement and success as soon as he arrived in the capital, the question of money remained, and no one had yet offered him a pension or permanent employment. So, a year after arriving in Paris, he accepted the offer to become secretary to the French ambassador in Venice. This was a clear advance in his fortunes yet, given that he had no experience or training for the job, his time in Venice was quite unhappy. The ambassador was incompetent and Rousseau lacked the bureaucratic demeanour that the job required. The evidence is unclear as to whether he quit or was fired but in either case he was free of his diplomatic responsibilities within a year. Yet his time in Venice had many benefits. For one, he was able to hear the best Italian music performed by the best ensembles for the first time, which affected his musical theory and composition in ways that would soon change his life. He said, 'I had brought from Paris the national prejudice against Italian music; but I had also received from nature that acute sensibility against which prejudices are powerless. I soon contracted the passion it inspires in all those born to understand it' (C 294).

Venice also sparked the first flames of his passion for social and political theory. In his brief life he had already lived in the Protestant city-state of Geneva, the new Catholic kingdom of Sardinia (which controlled Turin), the ancient Catholic kingdom of France and the dying Republic of Venice. These countries gave him a large supply of material from which to begin his political speculation. He later said, 'I had conceived the original idea for [a political treatise], at the time when I was in Venice and had some opportunity of observing the defects in that Republic's highly vaunted constitution.' His fundamental insight was that 'everything is rooted in politics and that, whatever might be attempted, no people would ever be other than the nature of their government made them' (C 377). Thus he began working on a manuscript that would come to fruition 20 years later in his treatise *The Social Contract*.

He soon returned to Paris and continued to work on his literary and musical projects while supplementing his income by giving music lessons and copying music, which at that time was still done by hand. It was soon after returning from Venice that he began one of the most unusual involvements of his life. Thérèse Levasseur was a poor young woman who did the laundry in Rousseau's Paris rooming house and lived with her father and rather unpleasant mother in a nearby slum. For reasons that are hard to explain, she and Rousseau found something attractive in one another and became lifelong partners, living together intermittently for the remainder of Rousseau's life and eventually marrying. Scholars have speculated at length about the psychological meaning of this union and the light it might offer on Rousseau's work, yet there is little consensus. For all their differences, however, the pairing was not as inexplicable as some have suggested. People who knew them both said that he was courteous and pleasant towards her and that she was not as simple-minded as one might suppose. While the surviving reports say that she was neither beautiful nor stimulating, they also say that he was hardly exceptional as a lover, friend and breadwinner. In any case, they gave each other some degree of domestic order and mutual affection, which apparently made up for the limitations that each must have found in the other.

In 1746, still lacking financial security, Rousseau accepted a job as secretary to the wealthy Dupin family, whom he had met through his aristocratic connections in Paris. For much of the next five years, he worked for them at their townhouse and especially at their country estate. The Dupins owned Chenonceau, one of the most famous and beautiful chateaux of the Loire valley. This Renaissance palace, which sits on the Cher River, consists of a tower on the riverbank with a long wing, supported by a series of roman-style arches, that spans the whole width of the river. The building faces on to two formal gardens, one laid out by King Henry II's wife Catherine de Medici, the other by his mistress Diane de Poitiers, which are surrounded by a large park. In this remarkable setting Rousseau composed songs, poems and a short play for performance at the chateau. He was also able to conduct research into chemistry and other natural sciences in a laboratory built by the Dupins.

The years with the Dupin family were important for other reasons, among which was the birth of Rousseau's first child. The number and fate of Rousseau's children with Mlle Levasseur is a matter of great controversy. The traditional story is that they had five children together, all of whom were abandoned in orphanages. This is the account that Rousseau gave in his autobiography and that others have repeated for centuries (C 333). Indeed, it circulated in his lifetime, and ever since then people with dreams of grandeur have tried to boost their credentials by claiming to be descended from one of his lost children. Yet there is evidence that the story is inaccurate and even perhaps that the children never existed; some scholars, for example, have suggested that Rousseau's health problems made him incapable of having children. This theory leaves the question of why he would have admitted to fathering and abandoning children if there never were any, and one obvious possibility is that Mlle Levasseur was not monogamous and Rousseau either did not know it or tried to protect her and himself from scandal. In any case, all of these interpretations face serious obstacles.

During this period Rousseau also began work on his contributions to the greatest publishing enterprise of the century, the *Encyclopedia*, which was then being planned by Denis Diderot and Jean d'Alembert. Rousseau had met Diderot soon after arriving in Paris and the two young men quickly became friends. Diderot was the more gregarious and urbane of the two, yet they were both poor sons of manual labourers and hoped to support themselves in Paris through their writings. They also shared interests in science, mathematics, art and social criticism. Soon after they met, d'Alembert asked Diderot to help him translate and edit an English encyclopedia of arts and sciences. Diderot accepted and, installing himself as the primary planner, significantly expanded the scope of the project to make it an original and comprehensive summary of philosophy, art, science and technology, which would not hesitate to present the most controversial ideas of the age.

The result was the *Encyclopédie, ou dictionnaire raisonné des sciences, des arts et des métiers*, published in 28 volumes between 1751 and 1772. (A new editor added seven more volumes later.) Diderot wrote, 'In truth, the aim of an encyclopedia is to collect all the knowledge that now lies scattered over the face of the earth, to make known its general structure to the men among whom we live, and to transmit it to those who will come after us, in order that the labour of past ages may be useful to the ages to come, that our grandsons, as they become better educated, may at the same time become more virtuous and more happy.' He commissioned Rousseau to write the articles on music, which he began to do in 1748.

Yet the most significant event in Rousseau's life during this period was the famous incident on the road to Vincennes in 1749, which was in many ways the decisive moment of his philosophical life. In July of that year Diderot was arrested following the publication of his 'Letter on the Blind', in which he defended a radical version of Locke's 'blank slate' thesis. Diderot argued that all ideas and many emotions derive from sense experience and reflection, rather than being innate in the soul. This theory seemed to challenge the orthodox belief that humans are innately sinful and also to undermine many proofs of the existence of God, which rely on the thesis that the idea of God is innate in the mind. Diderot was eventually transferred to house arrest in Vincennes outside Paris, where Rousseau often visited him. On one of these journeys he had the experience that gave the final shape to his philosophical outlook. His description of the incident offers an invaluable context for interpreting his mature philosophical work.

The summer of the year 1749 was excessively hot. Vincennes is some six miles from Paris. In no condition to pay for cabs, I walked there at two in the afternoon when I was alone, and I went fast so as to arrive early. The trees along the road, always lopped according to the custom of the country, hardly gave any shade; and often I was so prostrated with heat and weariness that I lay down on the ground, unable to go further. In order to slacken my pace I thought of taking a book with me. One day I took the *Mercure de France* and, glancing through it as I walked, I came upon this question propounded by the Dijon Academy for the next year's prize: Has the progress of the sciences and arts done more to corrupt morals or to improve them?

The moment I read this I beheld another universe and became another man. . . What I remember quite distinctly about this occasion is that when I reached Vincennes I was in a state of agitation bordering on delirium. Diderot noticed it. . . He encouraged me to give my ideas wings and compete for the prize. I did so, and from that moment I was lost. All the rest of my life and my misfortunes followed inevitably as a result of that moment's madness (C 327–28).

What was the new universe that he beheld? The beginning of the answer is contained in the essay question itself. It caused him to see that progress in science and art is not identical with moral progress, or that the extraordinary cultural development since the Renaissance may not have succeeded in making humanity any better or happier than it was before. In fact, it may have done the opposite. But why did this new idea have such an effect on him? It seems that prior to this moment on the road to Vincennes he had a number of partially formed insights that, in light of this new idea, suddenly became clear and began to fit into an overall picture of human life. He later summarized this picture in his famous phrase, 'the natural goodness of man'. While there is much that needs to be said about this phrase, the basic idea is clear enough. The human vices that make individuals unhappy and social life difficult are not simply the result of inherent human selfishness and cruelty; they are in some sense caused by social arrangements that bring out the worst in people.

The famous passage above has many other features worth mentioning. One important point is that it was written 20 years after the fact and, indeed, the earliest written account of that day is found in a letter composed by Rousseau in 1762. So over 12 years separate the event from the first telling of it, during which it probably came to have significance that it could not have had at the time. Indeed, the story seems so dramatically perfect, and so much like St Paul's experience on the road to Damascus, that some scholars believe it to be either entirely fictitious or at least highly coloured. Certainly his idea of reading while he walked simply in order to make himself go more slowly seems artificial. And one further piece of evidence seems to count against his reliability. The essay contest he mentions was announced in the October issue of the *Mercure de France*, which makes it hard to understand Rousseau's comment about the summer heat. But the evidence is far from definitive on either side. After all, October may have been unusually hot that year, or he may have taken up reading during the summer in order to slow down and continued to do it even after the weather cooled, or the issue of the *Mercure de France* may have been printed early. In any case, Diderot was imprisoned until November of that year, so the incident on the road to Vincennes may well have happened as he said.

One thing is indisputable. In the fall of that year Rousseau began writing his entry to the essay contest, in which he tried to express some of the insights that came to him by the roadside. The result was his first acknowledged masterpiece, 'Discourse on the Sciences and Arts', in which he argued that the progress of high culture since the Renaissance had made European civilization less happy and less moral. It made him famous throughout Europe, beginning in the summer of 1750 when the Dijon Academy awarded first prize to his essay. The acclaim that immediately descended upon him from France's intellectual class was perhaps unprecedented not merely in Rousseau's own life but in his whole century. He later wrote of the work, 'When I had won the prize Diderot undertook to get it printed; and whilst I was [ill] in bed he wrote me a note to inform me of its publication and reception. "It is taking on like wildfire," he announced, "There has never been a success like it." The public's kindness to an unknown author, which had not been intrigued for, gave me my first real assurance of my talents about which, despite my inner conviction, I had always been doubtful till then' (C 338–9).

One can barely imagine the effect of such recognition from the highest cultural circles of the most sophisticated capital in the world, offered to a runaway who less than two decades before had been employed as a penniless liveried footman in Turin. Yet this was merely the beginning of Rousseau's conquest of the French cultural scene in the mid-century. Beginning with the publication of his 'Discourse' and throughout the following 12 years, Rousseau achieved an unparalleled greatness both in the development of his own talent and in the public reception of his work. A number of incidents provide context for understanding the philosophical masterpieces he produced during this period.

In 1752 a musical company visited Paris to perform Italian comic opera, in particular Giovanni Pergolesi's *The Servant Mistress*. The visit was extremely controversial because, although there was a growing taste for this kind of music, Italian comic opera was about as different from classical French opera as anything could be. It had clear, beautiful melodies with simple accompaniment; its main characters were servants and artisans; it showed the lower classes getting the advantage of the higher ones; it was short; and it contained no ballet. Many music lovers in Paris, especially members of the aristocracy who favoured the highly formal operas of Rameau and his followers, intensely disliked Pergolesi's work. Yet it also found defenders, especially among the intellectual class. The quarrel that followed was one of the major cultural events of the century. Rousseau said, 'All Paris divided into two camps, whose excitement was greater than if they had differed over politics or religion. The more powerful and more numerous party, made up of the great, the rich, and the ladies, supported French music; the other, which was more active, more distinguished, and more enthusiastic, was made up of true music lovers, talented people, and men of genius (C 358). It is not hard to guess which side Rousseau took.

The first thing he did in taking up the cause of Pergolesi and Italian music in general was to complete an Italian-style opera of his own, but sung in French. It was not his first attempt at composing opera. He had written at least one previously while living with the Mablys in Lyon, which he destroyed before it was ever performed, and in Paris he had worked intermittently on his classical French opera, *The Gallant Muses*. The new opera was something quite different. Called *The Village Soothsayer*, it followed the Italian style in being a short, charming, highly melodic love story about shepherds in a rural village. Having written the libretto and composed the music himself, he premiered the work in the fall of 1752. It was an immediate sensation and was soon performed for the king, who liked it so much that he offered Rousseau a pension, which he refused. Rousseau later said that the opera, 'brought me completely into fashion, and soon no man in Paris was more sought after than I' (C 344). While the work has since fallen from the repertoire, its fame and impact at the time were enormous. Both Gluck and Mozart acknowledged its influence on their operas.

The next year Rousseau further enflamed the controversy by publishing his 'Letter on French Music'. In this work he argued that French music, and opera in particular, was essentially a debased form of aural communication. In particular, it confused the nature and purpose of music by deriving melody from harmony rather than the other way around. The pamphlet was a direct insult to Rameau, who had argued in his classic *Treatise on Harmony* that melody is a secondary feature of music that derives from underlying harmonic sequences built upon root notes. It may seem like an arcane debate, yet it reflected a clash of world views concerning language, culture, art and nature itself. Rousseau's essay became a primary battleground of the conflict, which quickly spread beyond the pages of magazines and books. He was hanged in effigy on the streets of Paris, and he later said that the war over his pamphlet averted a real civil war in France. The king had recently dissolved the Paris *parlement* in a controversy connected with Jansenism, and had thereby pushed his detractors towards open rebellion. Yet when Rousseau's essay was published all the anger was turned against him. 'My pamphlet appeared and immediately all other quarrels were forgotten; no one could think of anything except the threat to French music. The only revolt was now against me, and such was the outburst that the nation has never quite recovered from it' (C 358).

In the midst of this turmoil, in the fall of 1753, the Academy of Dijon announced another essay contest, this time on the question, 'What is the origin of inequality among men, and is it justified by natural law?' Rousseau's first 'Discourse' and the replies he had written to critics proved to him and to everyone else that he was a social theorist of the highest rank. Now, in response to the new essay question, he felt that he might be able to offer a truly revolutionary answer. He retired to the countryside and quickly produced his 'Discourse on the Origin and Foundations of Inequality', which marked a new epoch in the history of philosophy and perhaps in European civilization as a whole.

This work gave its readers a new way of understanding their own lives and the social world that surrounded them. Put simply, he argued that inequality is rooted in vanity and greed, which cause people to feel secret joy at the poverty and lowliness of others. This thesis by itself was not original because, as Rousseau knew, it had been defended a century before by the English philosopher Thomas Hobbes. The revolutionary part of Rousseau's theory was his claim that vanity and greed are not essential parts of human nature but are themselves the products of unjust social arrangements. Thus he was able to make good on his theory of 'the natural goodness of man' even in view of the obvious injustices and cruelties of the world around him. He interpreted them as a kind of corruption of an original human condition. In developing this insight he not only influenced the sciences of sociology and social psychology, but also set the foundation for a radically new political philosophy and educational theory.

The essay was too radical and too long for the judges of the Dijon Academy, who apparently did not even finish reading it. Yet Rousseau was famous by this time and had little trouble finding a publisher for this second 'Discourse', which appeared in 1755, the same year that he published the article 'Political Economy' in the fifth volume of the *Encyclopedia*. Although these works established his reputation throughout Europe as a leading political theorist, he felt himself increasingly at odds with the intellectual currents in Paris. Conservative thinkers opposed him because of his denial of original sin and his stinging criticism of French music. Yet he also did not fit comfortably with the progressive thinkers associated with the *Encyclopedia*. The thesis of his first 'Discourse', that the progress of high culture leads to unhappiness and moral decline, seemed to deny the basic principle of the *Encyclopedia*, which was that the spread of art, science and technology would improve human life indefinitely. He also found this group to be as greedy, vain, haughty and duplicitous as the aristocrats and clergymen whom they opposed. So when he finished his second 'Discourse' in 1754 he travelled to Geneva with a view to retiring there permanently.

It was an important trip for many reasons. For one, he visited Mme de Warens for the last time. They had become increasingly estranged since he moved to Paris, yet they corresponded occasionally and he sent her some of the earnings from his writing and musical composition, much to the dismay of Mlle Levasseur and her family. By this time Mme de Warens was in ill health and the visit was unpleasant for both of them. He later said, 'I saw her. In what a state, oh God! How low she had fallen! What was left to her of her former virtue?' (C 364). He travelled on to Geneva, and although Mme de Warens had been responsible for his conversion to Catholicism decades earlier, he reconverted as soon as he arrived back in his native city. His views on religion were now much more settled than they had been at his first conversion. He was certainly a theist and probably a Christian, yet he believed that the particular practices and dogmas of organized religion were arbitrary. He wrote of his decision, 'The Gospel being, in my opinion, the same for all Christians, and the fundamentals of dogma only differing over points that men attempted to explain but were unable to understand, it seemed to me to rest with the Sovereign alone in each country to settle the form of worship and the unintelligible dogma as well' (C 365).

In any case, after converting he regained his citizenship and could honestly call himself 'citizen of Geneva' as he had become accustomed to doing even while nominally a Catholic and so ineligible for citizenship. In the end he decided not to move to Geneva, in part because Voltaire had settled there. Although he had admired Voltaire as a young man, some hostility now existed between them because of the latter's snide response to Rousseau's theory of 'the natural goodness of man'. Eventually, Rousseau found a way to extricate himself from both Geneva and Paris. A wealthy friend offered him the use of a small house, the Hermitage, on an estate outside the French capital. Rousseau fell in love with the charming house and gardens the first moment he saw them, and he moved there with Mlle Levasseur and her mother in the spring of 1756. The next five years, first at the Hermitage and later at a second rural cottage, were the creative apogee of his life and constitute one of the greatest triumphs in the history of letters.

It is possible to mention only the highest peaks of his achievement during this period, which in fact began with a great disaster. In 1755 Portugal suffered an earthquake that killed thousands of people in and around Lisbon. In response, Voltaire wrote his famous 'Letter on the Lisbon Earthquake' arguing that such an event proves that there is no providential God overseeing human life. At almost the same time, in an unlucky coincidence, he sent a funny but mean letter to Rousseau about his second 'Discourse'. Rousseau responded as cordially as he could, yet Voltaire's ideas about both God and humanity were so much at odds with his own that his reply to Voltaire was nothing less than a fundamental criticism of the famous writer's world view. The text has come to be known as his 'Letter to Voltaire on Providence'. In it Rousseau argued that human beings, not God, had decided that people should live in tall buildings in crowded cities even in areas where earthquakes are common.

So, he asked, if an earthquake then destroys the city and people are injured because of their own choices, how does that disprove the existence of God? The letter was eventually made public in 1759, in response to which Voltaire published his famous parable *Candide* (C 400).

Rousseau's move to the countryside was directly responsible for another great work, the epistolary novel *Julie, or the New Heloise*. The beauty of his rural retreat stimulated Rousseau's memory and imagination in an extraordinary new direction. He began to write a story that took all of the most powerful events, people, places, emotions, ideas and ideals from his life and combined them into a single narrative. It is a story of love, duty, loss, family, education, science and art, all set in the country surrounding his beloved Lake Geneva. The main character is Julie, the daughter of an impoverished Swiss nobleman who hires a man named St Preux to be her tutor. St Preux was based on Rousseau himself, and the whole situation is similar to his experience as a tutor to the Mablys in Dijon. Julie and St Preux eventually become lovers, yet the father will not let them marry because he wants his daughter to make a match that will improve her fortune. He eventually arranges a union with Wolmar, an intelligent, wealthy, progressive landowner who lives on his successful estate nearby. Out of filial duty, Julie marries Wolmar, although she never loves him, and eventually the couple hire St Preux to tutor their own children. In the book's most famous scene, a sudden storm forces Julie and St Preux into a cove on Lake Geneva where they confess that their love has never died. But, rather than bring dishonour to her family, Julie decides that she must resist her passion for St Preux and be faithful to her husband. Not long afterwards she dies while saving her daughter from drowning in the lake. While the novel is little read today, it was an immense hit at the time. It went through 72 editions by 1800 and some scholars have calculated that it was the bestselling book of the eighteenth century.

Rousseau worked on *Julie* over a number of years and eventually published it in 1761. During this time he composed a series of additional masterpieces. In 1757 d'Alembert's article 'Geneva' appeared in the seventh volume of the *Encyclopedia*. As much as anyone, d'Alembert shared the conviction that progress in the arts and sciences improves human life, so he criticized Calvinist Geneva for its lack of high culture. He portrayed the city as somewhat dour and conservative and, in particular, he argued that the city should lift its ban on theatrical performances, stating that theatre tends to make its audience more thoughtful, sophisticated and tolerant, qualities that he believed were noticeably absent in Geneva. Rousseau responded with his 'Letter to d'Alembert on the Theatre', which further developed the theory of art and society that he had previously published in his first 'Discourse'.

While the letter was not a blanket rejection of the arts in general or theatre in particular, it offered a much less optimistic account of their influence on public morality than the one given by d'Alembert. Rousseau agreed that the theatre has an extraordinary effect on the character of its audience, but he thought it was generally a negative one. He singled out Molière as an example, saying that this playwright's subtle mockery of patriotism, simplicity and piety would undermine the civic virtues that every state relies on, especially a semi-democratic state like Geneva. The letter severed him completely from the main intellectual currents of Paris. Although his relationship with Diderot remained somewhat cordial, he gradually pulled himself away from the great thinkers of the capital and eventually came to believe that they had formed a cabal to discredit his ideas and slander his reputation, which in fact they had, although less so than he believed.

During these years Rousseau also composed the two books that were in many ways the culmination of his philosophical writing, *The Social Contract* and *Emile*. The full title of the first work was *Of the Social Contract, or Principles of Political Right* and it began where his second 'Discourse' left off. In the earlier work, he argued that political inequality comes neither from God nor from nature, but rather from human beings themselves who, in their desire to feel superior to others, create systems of domination and oppression, which they then formalize under the name of law and the state. Rousseau argued that such political societies, based merely on power, could never make a moral claim to the allegiance of their members. So, in *The Social Contract*, he offered an alternative ideal of a political system in which all citizens would be treated as free and equal, a system which would deserve the allegiance of its citizens because it would express their own will and promote the good of all.

Immediately after publishing *The Social Contract* in 1762, Rousseau published *Emile: Or on Education*, which he had completed at the same time. While he said of the two works that, 'together they make a kind of whole', it is hard to imagine books that differ more greatly in style and content. *Emile* is a long, didactic novel. While it begins as a recognizable treatise on education, not dissimilar from Locke's *Thoughts on Education*, it soon evolves into fictional narrative of the education of a young man named Emile by his tutor, Jean-Jacques. The educational programme that the tutor constructs is guided by a few simple principles, all of which appeared in Rousseau's earlier writing.

The most obvious of them is the idea that a person's mind and character are formed largely by the objects and people that he or she experiences in childhood. This was the same principle that Diderot employed in his controversial 'Letter on the Blind' and that Rousseau discussed in his second 'Discourse'. Here it forms the basis of an educational programme that carefully controls the experiences that Emile has from infancy through early adulthood, with the aim of making him a happy and useful adult. A second obvious principle guiding Emile's education is Rousseau's thesis of 'the natural goodness of man'. The programme is designed to encourage what is innately good in Emile rather than to beat out what is innately bad. A third principle is Rousseau's longstanding idea that vanity is the source of most unhappiness and cruelty. Emile is never allowed to enter a battle of wills with his tutor, and only gradually is he allowed to compare himself to people in wider society.

It is one of the most remarkable facts in the history of philosophy that two of the greatest works of the eighteenth century were written at the same time by a man in wretched health who was simultaneously writing the bestselling novel of the century, and furthermore that the two philosophical works were published within a month of each other. One can say that April and May of 1762 marked a new epoch in European thought. In many ways they marked a new epoch in all of history. For the influence of these two works was not confined to their extraordinary effect on the thought of Kant, Coleridge and other great thinkers of the late eighteenth century. They also had a great, if much debated, influence on the French Revolution and the great worldwide revolutions of the nineteenth century, and did much to provoke both neoclassicism and Romanticism as responses to the baroque style in literature, architecture, music and the visual arts. Whether Rousseau himself would have endorsed any of these developments is difficult to say.

RETREAT (1762–1778)

The last years of Rousseau's life were a bleak and stunning reversal from the heights of fame and influence that he had achieved in the 1750s. It was a period of debilitating illness, persecution, fear and, some say, madness. Yet in the midst of incredible hardship Rousseau created works that became important parts of his legacy. Even at the time, Rousseau knew that 1762 was the beginning of the final chapter of his life. By January of that year *The Social Contract* and *Emile* were in the hands of their publishers, and he had reason to suspect that their appearance would result in great persecution, for both works contained radical ideas on religion that he knew would distress the authorities in France and Geneva. He hoped that his friendship with the Director of Publications in France would spare him the worst of it, yet he was often warned that his unwillingness to publish his works anonymously would cause him great trouble. After reading a passage from the manuscript of *Emile* a friend wrote to him, 'My God, I tremble for you' (N 333). Some scholars puzzle over his stubbornness on this issue. He was after all familiar with the means of intimidation available to the state. Many of his friends had been jailed or otherwise persecuted for saying less radical things than he proposed in these two books and, in fact, both his second 'Discourse' and *Julie* had caused the political and ecclesiastical authorities to condemn him. He had avoided further persecution only by luck and the intervention of powerful friends.

Two things explain his behaviour in this period. The first is that, almost alone among his contemporaries, he put his name on all of his published work. He felt that it was part of his duty as a citizen to speak against injustice where he found it and to accept the consequences. Second, he was dying. For at least two years he had suffered debilitating pain and often lay on what he and others believed to be his deathbed. Indeed, part of the contract with the publisher of *The Social Contract* was that he would pay an annual annuity to Mlle Levasseur when Rousseau died. In a letter from this time he wrote, 'you must understand that in my present state of health it needs more candor than courage to tell the truths that are good for mankind, and from now on I can defy men to do their worst to me without having much to lose' (N 334). As it happened, he lived another 16 years.

Although *The Social Contract* was a book about politics and *Emile* was a book about education, the controversial issue in both cases was religion. In the chapter on civil religion in *The Social Contract* Rousseau argued that any infringement on freedom of conscience is an illegitimate use of state power, except when absolutely required for public safety. This alone was enough to upset the Catholic authorities in France, yet Rousseau went further. He said that one of the few legitimate constraints on the freedom of conscience is to outlaw Catholicism because the obedience that Catholics owe to the pope is incompatible with the obedience they owe to their civil magistrates. One can guess how such a doctrine was received. *Emile*, for its part, contained a long passage called the 'Profession of Faith of the Savoyard Vicar', in which a fictional Catholic priest defends a kind of natural religion. He says that there is no need for revelation or for Church hierarchy because each person's soul can reach out to God in its own way by contemplating the wonders of the natural world. The vicar not only denies the view that the Church is necessary for salvation, he also denies the truth of miracles, questions scripture and argues that organized religion is an actual hindrance to spirituality. The wonder is not that Rousseau was persecuted for these works; the wonder is that they were allowed to be published in the first place.

The struggle began almost immediately. *The Social Contract* and *Emile* were banned in France by the end of May. At first Rousseau was nonplussed, saying that a government has every right to ban books if it wanted to, and he would not object. Yet the Director of Publications, who understood the political scene in Paris better than Rousseau did, saw that anger against the books would soon turn to anger against their author. He sent a coded message to Rousseau urging him to flee France, but Rousseau refused in the somewhat naïve belief that his powerful friends could protect him. Finally, in early June, one of these benefactors sent a messenger in the middle of the night saying that the authorities in Paris planned to issue a warrant for his arrest the next morning. This caused him genuine fear, plus he saw that if the whole story of the books' publication were revealed it would endanger some of those protectors who had helped the works into print. So, the next morning he ran for the border, leaving Mlle Levesseur and his personal possessions under the protection of his remaining friends. Fleeing his home in a borrowed carriage, he passed the officers on their way to arrest him.

Over the following days he made a frightening journey through the French countryside and finally crossed the border into Swiss territory. He climbed from the carriage and kissed the ground. Yet other parts of Europe were no more welcoming. During the same spring the authorities in Geneva ordered *The Social Contract* and *Emile* to be burned. And while they refrained from actually issuing a warrant for Rousseau's arrest they declared that they would issue one if he ever again entered the city. At first he stayed in the Swiss territory of Berne, but he was soon ordered to leave there too. He then sought refuge in the lands of the king of Prussia, Frederick II (the Great), where he was welcomed by the king and especially by the local governor, who was an expatriate Scotsman. As the fall of 1762 approached, Rousseau was quite ill, but again he took up his pen. One vocal critic of *Emile* in France had been the Archbishop of Paris, Christophe de Beaumont. Although Beaumont was one of the chief critics of Rousseau and of the Jansenist movement, Rousseau respected his character if not his theology, and offered a detailed reply that was published the following year as his 'Letter to Beaumont'.

During this time, the political situation in Geneva was also extremely tense. For decades there had been tension between the major governing bodies in the city, which occasionally flared into civil unrest. Rousseau's condemnation by the city's leaders was itself an occasion for renewed conflict. One of the conservative leaders published a pamphlet called 'Letters Written from the Country' which defended the government and, implicitly, the actions it had taken against Rousseau. This same person had tried previously to have Rousseau stripped of his citizenship, so now he saw an opportunity for revenge and wrote his famous 'Letters Written from the Mountain'. It was another masterful piece of polemic. Rousseau accepted his critics' premises about the constitution of Geneva and then went on to show how the present government violated all of them. Moreover, he argued that the principles of government advocated by his critics were just those that he had defended in *The Social Contract*, which they had ordered to be burned.

In general, the next few years were pleasant for Rousseau. His health improved slightly, so he was able to resume his long walks in the countryside and to receive visitors, including the young James Boswell, who sought him out for spiritual and moral advice. He also took a number of small summer vacations among the beautiful alpine mountains and lakes. One very unusual opportunity came when a representative from Corsica arrived asking him to write the constitution for that nation, which had recently won its independence from Genoa. Although he never completed the project, he was pleased to be asked, and at his death he left behind a fascinating series of notes on the constitution. He also largely completed his *Dictionary of Music*, which he had been writing for years, partly based on the articles he had supplied for the *Encyclopedia*. A third project that occupied him was his great autobiography, *Confessions*. It seems that by the end of 1765 he had completed Part I, which told the story from his birth to his arrival in Paris in 1742. Yet this peaceful interlude did not last. His 'Letters Written from the Mountain' had caused anger and civil unrest not only in Geneva but throughout the surrounding Swiss territories. In September 1765 his house was stoned by an angry mob. He fled back to Berne, but the authorities there expelled him again.

He was hounded throughout Switzerland until, with very few options left, he decided to accept an invitation that had been given him when he first fled Paris. The great philosopher David Hume offered to bring him to England under his personal protection. Hume was an fervent admirer who, when asked by a third party to help Rousseau, said, 'there is no man in Europe of whom I have maintained a higher idea, and who I would be prouder to serve'. The friendship between the two greatest thinkers and writers of their generation was initially warm and reciprocal. Hume accompanied Rousseau to London, and once there found lodgings for him and solicited a pension from the English king. Rousseau was able to bring Mlle Levasseur to join him along with many of his manuscripts and letters. In a fairly quiet retirement outside London, Rousseau continued writing his *Confessions* and pursuing botany, which was the favoured hobby of his declining years. Yet a quarrel soon broke out.

One of Hume's friends, Horace Walpole, had written a cruel and not very funny document that purported to be a mocking letter to Rousseau from Frederick the Great. Rousseau believed that Hume encouraged its publication in England and on this basis formed the false idea that Hume was fomenting the same kind of mockery and persecution that Rousseau had fled on the Continent. There followed a public exchange of letters that showed both philosophers to be quite vain and self-righteous, although Rousseau appeared as the worse of the two. Some scholars have suggested that by this point he was suffering from a kind of mental breakdown and persecution complex. But it is worthwhile to remember that he had recently suffered five years of very real persecution during which his life and liberty were often in danger. In any case, he soon left Hume's company and returned to France.

Although he was technically a fugitive from justice, the French authorities did not arrest him. He spent a number of years roaming about France from the house of one friend to another, often under the pseudonym of Renou. He also made the surprising decision to marry Mlle Levasseur, although the union was in fact a 'declaration of mutual consent' rather than a real marriage, since the laws of France forbade Protestants from marrying Catholics. He also continued to write. In late 1767 he finally published his *Dictionary of Music* and soon afterwards received another solicitation for political advice, in response to which he wrote his 'Considerations on the Government of Poland'. His also finished the second part of his *Confessions*, which followed his life's story up to his departure for England in 1765. Although he did not publish the *Confessions* in his lifetime, he did give private readings to friends, and in the following centuries it came to be recognized as a masterpiece of literature, perhaps even the equal of its prototype by St Augustine. During this period he also wrote his 'Letters on Botany', which were published posthumously and much praised.

His final years were consumed by intense introspection, which resulted in two more autobiographical works. The first was *Rousseau, Judge of Jean-Jacques*, also known as his *Dialogues*. This book takes the elaborate form of a conversation between Rousseau and the public image of himself, 'Jean-Jacques'. Its purpose was to provide a correct image of himself for the public's mind that would, he hoped, replace the slanderous picture of him painted by his enemies. The tone of the books is querulous and frantic, no doubt because he wrote it during a period of great despair and paranoia. After completing it he attempted to place the manuscript on the high altar of Notre Dame in Paris.

In the autumn of that year, 1776, he was knocked down and injured by a large dog. While recovering he began to write his final work, which was left uncompleted at his death. His *Reveries of a Solitary Walker* takes the form of ten 'walks' in which he described his thoughts and feelings as he took long hikes around Paris recuperating from the incident with the dog. Largely autobiographical, with none of the self-righteousness of the *Dialogues*, it is one of his most acute and enduring works. The final walk is dated Palm Sunday 1778, the 50th anniversary of his first meeting with Mme de Warens. In May of that year he moved to a small cottage in Ermenonville outside Paris, where he died on 2 July. He was buried on the property, but his remains were transferred to the Panthéon in Paris during the French Revolution.

CHAPTER 2

'DISCOURSE ON THE SCIENCES AND ARTS'

Rousseau's first philosophical masterpiece, 'Discourse on the Sciences and Arts', was published in January 1751, when he was still an unknown émigré from Geneva living very modestly in Paris. Within a year of its appearance he had become one of the most celebrated writers in France. Many prominent thinkers of the time responded to the essay with praise or fascinated criticism, and it established him as a leading figure of mid-century intellectual life throughout Europe. Although the essay attacked the most fundamental beliefs of his contemporaries, it quickly became a touchstone of social criticism and has remained so to this day. It stunned its immediate audience, inspired later generations and still offers deep insights on human nature and social life. It is also a crucial text for understanding Rousseau's subsequent work because in this essay he first announced and defended the themes that ran through his later philosophical writing.

The essay's thesis, simply put, is that progress in art, science and technology tends to make human beings less virtuous and less happy, instead of more virtuous and more happy, with the implication that supposedly primitive civilizations are in fact better off than superficially advanced ones. Given that he wrote this while living in the most sophisticated capital of the era, it is not surprising that the common reaction was either outrage or amused curiosity. Indeed, he expected as much; in the Preface to the essay he wrote, 'I suspect I shall not easily be forgiven for taking the side I have dared to take. Clashing head on with all that is today admired by men, I can only expect universal blame' (D 4). Although the response of his contemporaries was not wholly negative, the essay did upset many people and it still retains its power to shock. The present age is perhaps more wary of science and technology and less enamoured of politeness and high culture than was Rousseau's, yet his thesis remains radical and striking.

BACKGROUND

To understand the argument of the 'Discourse' it is helpful to recall Rousseau's experience on the road to Vincennes in 1749, described in the previous chapter. On his way to visit Diderot he came across the advertisement for an essay contest on the theme, 'Has the restoration of the sciences and the arts contributed to the purification of morals?'. The wording of the question caused all of the fragmented insights and commitments he had developed throughout his unsettled life to come together suddenly into a comprehensive, vivid picture of human nature and society. This epiphany was the most important event in his philosophical life, and all of his major works flowed directly from the insights that he gained in that moment.

While his most famous description of the experience was written years later in his autobiographical *Confessions* (C 327), the earliest written testimony is from a letter of 1762 in which he described the event as follows. 'Suddenly I felt my mind dazzled by a thousand lights; a host of brilliant ideas sprang up together with such force and confusion that I was plunged into an inexpressible alxiety; I felt my head swim with a vertigo like drunkenness. A violent palpitation seized me and made me gasp for breath. . . I let myself drop under one of the trees of the avenue and there I spent half an hour of such agitation that when I got up I found the whole front of my jacket wet with tears I had shed unawares.'

In the same letter he went on to describe in outline the ideas that came to him in that moment. 'Oh, Monsieur, if I could have written even a quarter of what I saw and felt under that tree, with what clarity would I have revealed all the contradictions of our social system, with what force would I have exposed all the abuses of our institutions, with what simplicity would I have shown how man is naturally good, and it is only through their institutions that men have become bad' (N 325). In short, the vision he had on the road to Vincennes was of 'the natural goodness of man', or the idea that human suffering stems not from inherent evil in human nature but rather from social arrangements that suppress people's virtuous qualities and create destructive ones in their place. He wrote his

'Discourse' in the weeks following this incident, and, while it was only his first attempt to explain and defend this radical new vision of human life, the result was stunning. In the end, the Academy awarded his essay first prize.

One of the difficulties for understanding the essay is that the Academy's original question was more complicated than it first appears; furthermore, Rousseau went on to shape it in ways different than the Academy probably intended. So all of this must be clarified before the reader can approach the 'Discourse' from the right direction. The first and most vexing issue has to do with the use of the word 'morals' in the wording of the question. The English word 'morals' is the typical translation of the French *moeurs*, which is the word the Academy used. Yet the French word has different connotations than the English, because in addition to the plain idea of 'morality', it also takes in the whole realm of manners, habits and customs. So, for example, to ask about the *moeurs* of a certain group is to ask not only about its morality in the narrow sense but also about its whole way of life.

In this sense *moeurs* is obviously similar to the English 'mores', yet even here the scope of the two terms is not identical and the connotations are certainly different. For in French it is common to discuss the *moeurs* of an animal species, for example, as in English one would discuss its 'behaviour', which shows how different the term is from both the English terms 'morals' and 'mores'. One consequence is that there is no unambiguous way to discuss *moeurs* in English, so in the following I will sometimes leave it untranslated and hope that the reader understands that it covers morals, manners, habits, customs and institutions. The important point is that the Academy's question is not quite what it first appears to be in English because, in asking whether progress in the sciences and arts has purified *moeurs*, they asked not simply whether it has made people morally better but whether it has helped to create better and more satisfying habits, customs and institutions. It is impossible to grasp Rousseau's meaning without keeping this in mind.

Yet the difficulties do not end there, because many of the other words cause similar problems. The phrase 'sciences and arts', *les sciences et les arts*, is also troublesome because these terms have a range of meanings that is quite different from what the reader might expect, especially the word *arts*. In Rousseau's milieu the word *art* meant something close to craft, or technology, or know-how. This is quite different from the modern idea of 'fine arts' such as painting, sculpture and theatre. Yet the word *art* could encompass the fine arts too, which only adds to the confusion, especially because in Rousseau's time many people thought of the fine arts largely as a matter of technique or craftsmanship rather than a matter of creative genius or some such thing. Thus, the phrase 'the sciences and arts' includes all aspect of intellectual culture from painting and theatre, to the natural and social sciences, to engineering and medicine.

In sum, the question of whether the restoration of *les sciences et les arts* has purified *moeurs* is the question of whether the growth of creativity, knowledge and technology since the Renaissance has caused an improvement in the overall way of life of European civilization. This is the question Rousseau set out to answer, and it explains why his essay ranges so far beyond science and art, and so far beyond morality, in the narrow sense of the English words. Yet it is also important to see that, even with this background, the Academy's question is ambiguously worded. The question, 'Has the restoration of the sciences and arts contributed to the purification of morals?' could mean at least two different things. It could assume that morals have been purified and then ask whether the restoration of the sciences and arts caused it. Or, it could ask whether this purification has happened at all. Rousseau, for one, took it in the latter way.

Finally, however, even if he interpreted their question correctly, his answer went well beyond what the Academy asked, because the appropriate response should presumably have been either 'yes' the sciences and arts have improved life or 'no' they have left it where it was. Yet Rousseau exploded this framework by going on to argue that the sciences and arts, far from being either beneficial or neutral, have actually made things worse. They have not only failed to improve the human situation, they have positively harmed it. Thus at the beginning of the 'Discourse' he subtly misquotes the Academy in order to change the terms of the debate. He faithfully transcribes their question, 'Has the restoration of the sciences and the arts contributed to the purification of morals?', but then quietly adds, 'or to their corruption?'(D 5). This change, which gave a new and decisive meaning to the question, allowed him to advance a thesis that was probably not even imagined by the people who proposed the issue to which he was supposedly responding.

THE ARGUMENT

The 'Discourse' is divided into two main parts supplemented by brief footnotes and prefatory materials, some of which were included in the original essay he submitted to the Academy and some added only when it was published the following year. The first part of the essay attempts merely to establish a historical fact: that every time there has been an advance in the sciences and arts, it has been accompanied by a parallel corruption of *moeurs*. The second part of the essay is analytical rather than simply descriptive. It tries to establish a link between the two phenomena by arguing that the advance in science and art actually causes a corruption in morals and customs. The reader will note that in both parts of the essay the evidence is thin and the inferences are loose. Rousseau himself admitted that the argument sometimes lacks precision and structure. In his *Confessions* he said that the essay, 'though full of strength and fervour, is completely lacking in logic and order. Of all those that have proceeded from my pen it is the most feebly argued, and the most deficient in proportion and harmony' (C 329). This may over-state the essay's weakness, but the work is certainly difficult to follow in places. However, its basic two-part structure can help the reader navigate the involved and sometimes convoluted argument.

First he tries to show that, whenever science and art have advanced, morals and customs have become debased. In his some-what elaborate phrasing, 'The daily rise and fall of the Ocean's waters have not been more strictly subjected to the course of the Star that illuminates us by night, than has the fate of morals and probity to the progress of the Sciences and Arts. Virtue has been seen fleeing in proportion as their light rose on our horizon, and the same phe-nomenon has been observed at all times and in all places' (D 9). The support for such a claim must come from relevant historical evi-dence, of course, so in the remainder of the first part of the essay he goes on to present a brief survey of the growth and decline of great civilizations, including Egypt, Constantinople, China and especially Greece and Rome. He claims that their history proves that there is an inverse relationship between science and art on the one hand and virtue and happiness on the other.

The most obvious question about Part I is what he meant by virtue and happiness. Or, to put it more precisely, the essay needs to explain what good morals, habits, manners and customs are as opposed to bad ones; one cannot judge the purity or corruption of a society's *moeurs*, and speculate about its causes, without some relevant standard of what it means to have pure *moeurs*. Here, unfortunately, Rousseau was not as explicit as the subject warrants. Yet one can sift through his comments about past and present civilizations to extract a fairly clear sense of the values that guided him. Roughly speaking, he thought of good *moeurs* as a matter of martial, civic virtue. This is clearest perhaps in his comparison between ancient Sparta and Athens, where he portrayed rustic simplicity and urban sophistication at their extremes, and came down clearly on the side of the former. 'O Sparta! Eternal shame to a vain teaching! While the vices, led by the fine Arts, together insinuated themselves into Athens, while a Tyrant was there so carefully assembling the works of the Prince of Poets, you expelled the Arts and Artists, the Sciences and Scientists from your walls' (D 11).

His vision of a good society was built from a diverse cluster of values and customs, which included simplicity, honesty, frugality, diligence, sincerity, courage, integrity, public spiritedness, self-government and military strength. He did not try to defend these values, nor did he explain how they are related or how they should be ranked with respect to each other. Instead, in Part I he makes the more modest, historical argument that where the sciences and arts have advanced, these qualities have always declined. Near the end of the section he summarizes this line of thought by saying that 'luxury, dissoluteness and slavery have at all times been the punishment visited upon our prideful efforts to leave the happy ignorance into which eternal wisdom had placed us' (D 14). In Part II he goes beyond this merely historical observation to claim that the advance of the sciences and arts not only accompanies a decline in morals, customs and institutions, but actually causes it.

The logic in the second part is not always clear because it traces causal chains that run along many different lines and interact in a variety of complicated ways. It is probably impossible to make a perfectly rational reconstruction of Rousseau's theory on these points. Yet a few aspects of his argument are unmistakable and form significant parts of his overall social theory. In particular, he describes four clear and direct ways that the sciences and arts corrupt *moeurs*. For a start, they cause a loss of time and labour that could be put to better use. 'Born in idleness', he says, 'they feed it in turn; and the irreparable loss of time is the first injury they necessarily inflict on society. In politics, as in ethics, not to do good is a great evil, and every useless citizen may be looked upon as a pernicious man' (D 17). He even claims that this charge should be brought against the great figures of modern science such as Kepler, who discovered the laws of planetary motion, and Newton, who discovered the law of universal gravitation. 'Answer me, I say, you from whom we have received so much sublime knowledge; if you had never taught us any of these things, would we have been any the less numerous for it, any the less well governed, the less formidable, the less flourishing or the more perverse?' (D 17).

A second way that science harms society is that when its theories are wrong or incomplete, which is more often than not, it can produce greater errors than if the theory had never been proposed in the first place. 'How many dangers! How many wrong roads in the investigation of the Sciences? Through how many errors, a thousand times more dangerous than the truth is useful, must one not make one's way in order to reach it? The drawback is manifest; for false-hood admits of an infinite number of combinations; but truth has only one way of being' (D 16–17). He did not offer any examples of injuries caused by false scientific theories and, in fact, it would be interesting to know what he had in mind. The reader today is all too familiar with the dangers of incomplete theories and misunderstood technological discoveries, yet one wonders what were the equivalent examples in the eighteenth century.

A further harmful effect of the sciences and arts, he argues, is that they cause a decline in martial virtue by encouraging people to be meek and cerebral. 'While the conveniences of life increase, the arts improve, and luxury spreads; true courage is enervated, the military virtues vanish, and this too is the work of the sciences and of all the arts that are practiced in the closeness of the study' (D 20). In par-ticular he cites the Romans, who 'admitted that military virtue died out among them in proportion as they began to be knowledgeable about Paintings, Etchings, Goldsmith's vessels, and to cultivate the fine arts' (D 21), as well as the Greeks in the time of their ascen-dancy, of whom he says, 'The ancient Republics of Greece, with the wisdom that was most conspicuous in most of their institutions, had forbidden their citizens the exercise of all those quiet and sedentary occupations which, by allowing the body to grow slack and cor-rupted, soon enervated the vigor of the soul. How, indeed, can men overwhelmed by the least need and repelled by the least pain be expected to face up to hungers, thirsts, fatigues, dangers, and death' (D 21).

Related to the loss of time and military virtue is his fourth argument, that the sciences and arts make people petty and trivial, which is to say that they encourage people to worry about unimportant things while ignoring what is really significant. 'This is the most obvious effect of our studies, and the most dangerous of all their consequences. People no longer ask about a man whether he has probity, but whether he has talents; not about a Book whether it is useful, but whether it is well written. Rewards are lavished upon wits, and virtue remains without honors' (D 23). He argues that after sufficient time people come to see this cultivated pettiness as the pinnacle of human achievement and the whole point of education. 'From our very first years a senseless education adorns our mind and corrupts our judgment. Everywhere I see huge establishments, in which young people are brought up at great expense to learn everything except their duties. Your children will not know their own language, but will speak others that are nowhere in use. . . they will not know the meaning of the words magnanimity, equity, temperance, humanity, courage; the sweet name Fatherland will never strike their ear' (D 22).

He argues that one aspect of this pettiness is especially harmful, namely the concern for luxury and ostentation over virtue. While the analysis of the social consequences of wealth was much more fully developed in his later works, especially his second 'Discourse', the core of the theory was present in the earlier essay. He argues that when a society's attention is turned from simplicity and public-spiritedness to less important things such as wit, outward appearance and style, money comes to be seen as valuable because, while one cannot buy virtue, one can buy rare and pretty things. Thus, he asks, 'what will become of virtue when one has to get rich at all cost? The ancient politicians forever spoke of morals and of virtue; ours speak only of commerce and of money' (D 18). He summarizes this line of argument by saying, 'A taste for ostentation is scarcely ever combined in one soul with a taste for the honest. No, Minds debased by a host of futile cares cannot possibly ever rise to anything great; and even if they had the requisite strength they would lack the courage' (D 19).

Roughly speaking, then, this is the line of causality he traced. The arts and sciences cause people to waste time and develop a desire for luxury and riches. This in turn corrupts morals, in the narrow sense, by causing people to be petty, selfish, duplicitous and dishonest, which in turn corrupts *moeurs* generally by creating a society of clever deceivers whose manners may appear to be exquisitely refined, but exist only to hide the selfish character within, all of which leads to a debased taste in culture and to tyrannical and oppressive political institutions. 'This is how the dissolution of morals, the necessary consequence of luxury, in turn leads to the corruption of taste' (D 20).

The obvious implication of his argument is that the societies that seem the most advanced will also be those whose members are least moral and least happy. This means in turn that people who genuinely wish to serve humanity should not promote the sciences and arts. In fact, he reserved his most biting criticism for those who interpret high culture for a general audience. 'But if the progress in the sciences and the arts has added nothing to our genuine felicity; if it has corrupted our morals, and if the corruption of morals has injured purity of taste, what are we to think of that crowd of Popularizers who have removed the difficulties which guarded the access to the Temple of the Muses, and which nature had placed there as a trial of the strength of those who might be tempted to know?' (D 26). One quakes to think what he would have said about the present book and its author.

In any case, one final distinction is crucial to understand Rousseau's point correctly, and it will prevent the reader from falling into an error that has trapped many critics of his 'Discourse'. His criticism of the sciences and arts was not a denunciation of science and art as such – rather it was an analysis of the harmful affects that they have on most or all societies in which they flourish. This may seem like a distinction without a difference, yet it is in fact an essential aspect of his theory. He did not at all promote a kind of know-nothingness or anti-intellectualism. He repeatedly said in the essay that science and philosophy are noble in themselves and potentially good for society at large. He praised great figures such as Plato, Cicero and Francis Bacon, not only for their cultural achievements but also for their beneficial effects on the wider world, and he argued that such people should be encouraged in their discoveries. 'Let kings therefore not disdain admitting into their councils the people most capable of counseling them well . . . Let learned men of the first rank find honorable asylum in their courts. Let them there receive the only reward worthy of them; by the credit they enjoy, to contribute to the happiness of the Peoples to whom they will have taught wisdom. Only then will it be possible to see what virtue, science, and authority, animated by a noble emulation and working in concert for the felicity of Mankind, can do' (D 27).

These passages show that Rousseau's point was not really about science and art at all, or even about scientists and artists. It concerned the effects that the sciences and arts as cultural institutions have on the societies in which they grow. Even readers in his own time failed to make this distinction. One early critic of his 'Discourse' was Stanislas Leszinski, the deposed king of Poland and father to the queen of France, who in a 'Reply' to the 'Discourse' criticized Rousseau for failing to see the nobility and value of the sciences. Rousseau published 'Observations' on this 'Reply' in which he reiterated and clarified his argument saying, 'Science in itself is very good, that is obvious; and one would have to have taken leave of good sense, to maintain the contrary'. The problem, he continued, is its effect on society at large. He asked, 'how does it happen that the Sciences, so pure in their source and so praiseworthy in their end, give rise to so many impieties, so many heresies, so many errors, so many absurd systems, so many vexations, so much foolishness?' The 'Discourse' was his answer to the question, and he concluded this part of his response to Leszinski by saying, 'My Adversary, for his part, admits that the Sciences become harmful when they are abused and that many do indeed abuse them. In this we are not, I believe, saying such very different things; I do, it is true, add that they are much abused, and that they are always abused, and it does not seem to me that the contrary has been upheld in the Answer' (D 33).

There does, however, seem to be a change in his argument between the 'Discourse' and his reply to Leszinski, because he had initially suggested that the sciences are founded on human vanity and laziness, whereas in the latter he says that they derive from a noble desire to understand God's creation. This contradiction is not quite as it appears, however, because in both works he made an implicit distinction between two ways of doing science and two kinds of scientists, a distinction that clarifies many of the apparent contradictions in his argument. He drew a line between the great original thinkers such as Plato and Bacon on the one hand, and the lesser minds who develop the institutions and customs of intellectual culture. His praise of science was always directed at the great thinkers themselves, while his argument against high culture was really against the effects of its popularizers. Thus his point was not that intellectual culture itself is bad, but that 'since the Sciences harm morals more than they benefit society, it would be preferable to have men pursue them less eagerly' (D 34).

In this light, his thesis was both less and more radical than it first appears. It was less so in the sense that his vision of a good society was not merely of a collection of simple, rustic warriors living in huts and conquering their neighbours, because he admitted the value of a life of the mind both for certain individuals and also for the societies they inhabit. His analysis of the early Roman republic and the Scythians, to take two obvious examples, showed that military virtue and high culture do not mix; but this does not mean that these rustic, bellicose societies should be, in his view, the highest aspiration of human civilization. Whatever he advocated, it was not a return to ignorance, superstition and violence. He explicitly said that during the medieval period, for example, Europe had 'relapsed into the Barbarism of the first ages' and that this condition was even worse than his contemporary society (D 6). And even in his discussion of Sparta, which he often held up as a perfect city, he was finally forced to say that it was 'in truth monstrous in its perfection' (D 22, note). In this sense the final point of the 'Discourse' was more moderate and conciliatory than it first appears.

Yet the argument was also quite radical, because Rousseau's distinction between great thinkers and creators on one side, and everybody else on the other, seems to divide all of humanity into two types or grades: those who can and will make permanent contributions to human civilization, and those who cannot. The former will contribute to intellectual culture regardless of the circumstances, and the latter are better off living in simplicity and piety. If this is what he meant to say, however, then it is a radical theory indeed. It is radical in its assessment of human potential and its limits, but even more so in its political implications. For it is unclear how these two groups, the best and the rest, could occupy the same society. The high culture of the elites is always in danger of corrupting the *moeurs* of the masses, but without the elites the masses will live in poverty, ignorance and barbarism. There is therefore a serious dilemma about how society should be organized.

Plato's *Republic* offered one solution, so it is not surprising to find Rousseau praising that work in his 'Discourse' (D 19). However, the means that Plato suggested to unite intellectual sophistication in the leaders with simplicity and piety in the general populace were radical in the extreme and repellent to most readers. The techniques advocated in the dialogue (although Plato himself may not have endorsed them) include systematic deception of citizens with the so-called 'noble lie', the assassination of political opponents, the suppression of dissidents by a 'nocturnal council', the confiscation of private property, the kidnapping of children, and a sophisticated eugenics programme. This makes one ask whether Rousseau had something similar in mind. He did not explicitly recommend such measures, of course, and his own political masterpiece, *The Social Contract*, defends a vision of politics at odds with Plato on many points. Yet his distinction between great minds and everyone else, along with his praise of Plato in the 'Discourse' and elsewhere, suggests that many of the most extreme elements of Plato's political philosophy swim somewhere not far below the surface of Rousseau's 'thought'.

In any case, Rousseau's overall thesis was that the development of art, science and technology causes the corruption of morals in a broad sense. It creates a society of lazy, selfish, petty, cowardly, dishonest and, in the end, unhappy people. This argument challenged some of the basic commitments of his contemporaries, many of whom took it for granted that the progress of intellectual culture, and especially the progress of technology, would improve human life indefinitely. They assumed that as humanity's power to control and manipulate nature increased, people would be able to shape the world to fit their wants and needs. And they believed that development of medicine, engineering, clinical psychology, educational theory and other such fields would necessarily make human life more pleasant, refined and satisfying.

There are good reasons to accept this view, of course. The more one understands nature, including human nature, the more one can control it; and the more one can control it, the more one can improve human existence. The logic seems simple and almost inevitable even today in a world that has experienced technological horrors unimagined by the eighteenth-century champions of progress. Yet Rousseau denied the proposition at its root. He argued that technology, and intellectual culture generally, cannot provide the things that make life satisfying, such as friendship, integrity and public service, and indeed that they erode the very elements of human well-being while pretending to supply them.

THE RESPONSE

When the 'Discourse' was finally published in 1751, the response was explosive. It angered almost every possible readership and even those on opposite ends of the major issues of the time found common cause in rejecting its arguments. The most conservative religious thinkers joined with the most radical philosophers in condemning Rousseau's thesis of 'the natural goodness of man' and his analysis of the harms of high culture. Yet it also produced a kind of amused curiosity, especially among the most sophisticated of his readers such as Diderot and Voltaire. The ensuing controversy and Rousseau's response to it clarifies his intentions in a number of different ways. In particular his restatement, and in some cases his revision, of his position in various letters to critics is very helpful in discerning what exactly he intended to argue for.

His theory of 'the natural goodness of man' was controversial for two opposite reasons. On one side were the defenders of orthodox Christianity. From their perspective, his argument denied the doctrine of original sin and thereby rendered meaningless the suffering, death and resurrection of Jesus Christ. If people are not marked by original sin, then they do not need a supernatural redeemer to make them good and happy and acceptable in the eyes of God; they only need the right social institutions to cultivate their natural goodness. Thus, they viewed Rousseau's argument as a direct assault on Christianity, whether or not he intended it as such. Moreover, his timing was especially bad because at that moment the nature of original sin was one of the most controversial theological issues. The story of how this came to be helps clarify Rousseau's theory and the extraordinary response to it in the early 1750s.

In the previous century many French Catholics had become followers of Cornelius Jansen, Bishop of Ypres, who offered a radical argument about sin. Based on his reading of St Augustine he proposed that after the Fall human nature had become so depraved by sin that it was now impossible for anyone to earn salvation, no matter how outwardly virtuous they might appear. A person could not earn it through pious acts because all human deeds are tinged with sinfulness, nor could the Church award it to the faithful. Eternal salvation could come, if it came at all, only as a free gift of God's mercy to people who were in no way deserving of it. This view won the support of many great theologians of the time, including

Arnauld and Pascal, yet it was also very controversial among Catholics, not least because it seemed dangerously similar to the theologies of Martin Luther and especially John Calvin. Furthermore, if Jansen was correct that there is nothing anyone can do to earn salvation, then it seemed to render the Church itself useless or, at least, it meant that the Church could not claim to affect the salvation of its members.

Faced with this challenge, the Catholic cause was taken up by the Jesuits, who argued that although humans are innately sinful, they could render themselves worthy before God by means of good works and the power of the Church's sacraments. The controversy between the Jansenists and Jesuits was one of the major events of French cultural life in the seventeenth century and produced many important works of theology, most notably Pascal's *Provincial Letters*, which are still regarded as perhaps the greatest masterpiece of French philosophical prose. Eventually, however, the Jesuits won. Jansenism was declared a heresy and its spiritual centre, the convent at Port-Royal-des-Champs, was razed. Yet the conflict lingered in Rousseau's time and he himself was very influenced by Jansenist writers, even though he rejected their theory of innate human depravity. The situation was further complicated because, by the middle of the eighteenth century, the Jesuits had themselves greatly irritated the French monarchy over other issues, with the result that they were finally expelled from the country.

Thus, Rousseau's denial of original sin arrived just at the moment when it would create the greatest anger and irritation, unacceptable as it was to the partisans of the Jesuits and Jansenists alike, who now rounded on a common enemy. Despite their differences over the question of sin and grace, both parties agreed that the meaning of Christ's life and death rested on the doctrine of original sin. Indeed, Rousseau's ideas seemed to revive the ancient heresy of Pelagianism, which the Catholic Church had repeatedly crushed during the previous centuries. The fifth-century monk Pelagius had argued that the doctrine of original sin was incompatible with God's justice, because a just God would not punish people for sins that they could not help committing. Original sin also seemed to undermine free will; if people cannot help sinning then they are ultimately not free to choose how to live and thus to merit salvation. To him this meant either that God is unjust or that humans are not inherently sinful and, faced with the choice, he took the latter option and rejected the theory of original sin, saying that later generations did not auto-matically inherit Adam's guilt. Pelagius had been excommunicated more than a millennium before, but now it appeared as though his theory had found new life in Rousseau's 'Discourse'.

Yet while Rousseau faced criticism from orthodox Catholics and Jansenists alike, his essay was also at odds with the most influential theories of human nature at the time, especially that of the seventeenth-century English philosopher Thomas Hobbes, who was himself anti-clerical and perhaps even an atheist. Rousseau's philosophical works were often point-by-point arguments against Hobbes, and this is true of the first 'Discourse', which was implicitly intended to refute Hobbes's theory of human nature. In fact, one of his examples of the dangers of technology is that the invention of the printing press will allow Hobbes's works to live forever (D 25–6). While Hobbes had little to say about original sin, he argued for a fairly pessimistic view of human nature and, like many religious con-servatives, he defended an authoritarian view of politics according to which the state could and should do whatever it can to keep the peace, even at the price of denying civil liberties.

According to Hobbes's theory of human nature, people are moti-vated by a small set of basic emotions, the most important of which are vanity and fear of violent death, which in turn put people into fundamental conflict with one another. The fear of death causes them to lash out in preemptive violence against each other, because each one calculates that it is better to strike first instead of waiting to be attacked. And vanity causes them to take pleasure in the suffering of others, so even if there were no strategic advantage to harming other people, they would do it anyway just to feel superior. This account of human psychology is the background to Hobbes's theory that, without the coercive power of government, human society would be 'a war of every man against every man' in which the life of each person is 'solitary, poor, nasty, brutish, and short'.

On this basis he developed a political theory according to which the first purpose of the state should be to prevent people from harming one another, and that this end justifies any means necessary to achieve it. Hobbes was an extraordinarily controversial figure in Rousseau's time, although not because of his expansive view of political authority, which many defenders of the French monarchy found congenial. Rather, he had a negative view of organized reli-gion and Catholicism in particular. While his religious opinions were complicated and are much debated today, one point is undisputed. He thought that since political order could only be achieved if there is a single set of clear and enforced laws, religion poses a great political danger because it offers an alternative set of rules that might conflict with those of the civil authorities. He resolved this dilemma by denying any political authority to religious leaders, arguing that 'the ministers of Christ in this world, have no power by that title, to punish any man for not believing, or for contradicting what they say'. In this regard, Hobbes's views could not have been further from those of many Catholics, yet Rousseau's argument challenged both views by denying that human beings are inherently acquisitive, aggressive and vain.

Hobbes's influence in eighteenth-century France is much debated. Yet it is obvious that Rousseau developed his major arguments in response to Hobbes and that many of his readers had a roughly Hobbesian view of human nature in mind when they objected to his theory of 'the natural goodness of man'. Yet his point of criticism of Hobbes was more complicated than it might seem, for while he certainly rejected Hobbes's theory of human nature, he did so in a nuanced way. Rousseau did not deny that people are largely as Hobbes described them. Rather, he claimed that these traits are the result of social institutions, not inevitable parts of human nature. In other words, societies that have embraced the sciences and arts along with their attendant institutions will produce people who are very much as Hobbes described them. But, he argued, this says more about the effects of the sciences and arts on human *moeurs* than it does about human nature itself. In short, Rousseau believed that, since history offers examples of both extraordinary virtue and miserable vice, their causes must be sought not in human nature alone, which is obviously capable of both, but rather in external forces, especially social forces, that shape people in one way or the other.

Yet Rousseau's powerful argument against Hobbes opened him up to another fundamental objection, which was first raised by d'Alembert in the 'Preliminary Discourse' to the *Encyclopedia*. He said that whereas Rousseau put the blame for human vice solely on the sciences and arts, he should have looked to other forces such as politics and economics. His answer to this objection was less successful, saying only that 'the very hidden but very real relations between the nature of government on one hand, and the genius, morals, and knowledge of the citizens on the other, would have to be examined; and this would involve me in delicate discussions that might lead me too far' (D 39).

Yet he would not need to disagree fundamentally with d'Alembert, for his 'Discourse' is based on the idea that there is mutual inter-action between social institutions and individual character. The sciences and arts are an important aspects of social life, but not the only ones. So, to make his case that science and art corrupt *moeurs*, he need not show that they are the only things that corrupt *moeurs*, or that they do it independently of political circumstances. On the contrary, the root of his argument is that the sciences and arts tend to affect the character of both individuals and institutions, and that all three of these (the individual, social institutions and the state) shape each other in complicated ways. In any case, he went on to develop these ideas more fully in his 'Discourse on the Origin and Foundations of Inequality'.

Behind these objections, however, there is a more perplexing, and more interesting question, which concerns not the coherence of the argument but rather its motivation. If Rousseau believed that intellectual culture is bad for society, how could he justify his own activity as a musical composer and a philosopher? This is a telling issue, and it is important to frame it correctly. One might first recall his distinction between great thinkers on the one hand and the social institutions of high culture on the other. He argued that the former are very good and the latter very bad. In this light, one might believe that he counted himself among the great thinkers, like Bacon and Newton, whose philosophical work benefited both themselves and the societies in which they lived. His intellectual activity would thus be justified by the elevation it brought to his own mind and by the good it allowed him to do in the world. But this interpretation is implausible. To begin with, the 'Discourse' was written for a learned academy that was just the kind of institution that he thought harmed society by bringing high culture to a wider audience. Furthermore, he later agreed to have it published, which made it available to anyone who wished to read it. So the question remains of how his principles could justify his participation in the high culture of his time.

To some extent, they could not. After Rousseau's experience on the road to Vincennes, he began a deliberate programme of reform in his lifestyle to make it more consistent with his moral commitments. He said that when he heard that he had won the Academy's prize, the news 'reawakened all the ideas that it had suggested to me, endowed them with fresh vigour, and set that first leavening of heroism and virtue working in my heart that my father, my native land, and Plutarch had implanted there in my childhood. I could no longer see any greatness or beauty except in being free and virtuous'. Thus he resolved to change his habits. 'Although false shame and fear of opprobrium prevented me at first from acting on these principles and from openly defying the conventions of my age, my mind was made up from that moment' (C 332). Beginning in the mid-1750s he composed less music, moved out of Paris, attended fewer salons, began wearing rustic clothes, stopped carrying a sword and in general tried to bring his life into alignment with the virtues that he professed, which meant he would no longer participate in the kinds of institutions that he criticized in his 'Discourse'.

So, one way to interpret the apparent contradiction between his criticism of high culture and his contribution to it is simply to say that it was a contradiction. And perhaps he never resolved it, because he continued both to criticize high culture and to write books until the very end of his life. He said as much himself, especially in reference to his novel *Julie*, which he wrote in the late 1750s. It is an epistolary and somewhat didactic novel – in the style of Samuel Richardson's *Pamela* and *Clarissa* – which contains minute analyses of human emotions, especially romantic love. It is, in other words, the least likely book to have been written by the great follower of Plutarch and defender of Sparta against Athens. He felt the contradiction, yet could not stop the flow of emotion and creativity.

> My chief embarrassment was shame at so fully and openly going back on myself. After the strict principles that I had just proclaimed with so much noise, after the austere rules that I had so loudly preached, after so much stinging invective against effeminate books which breathed of love and languor, could anything more unexpected or more shocking be imagined than that I should suddenly with my own hand enroll myself among the authors of these books I had so violently censured? (C 404).

Yet there is more involved in his decision to keep writing, and to publish his writing, than a mere lack of willpower. For although he believed that the sciences and arts generally made people immoral and unhappy, he also thought they could be beneficial if used correctly. The more obvious way this can be so, discussed above, is that people of superior intellect might become advisers to political leaders. Yet this is irrelevant to Rousseau's case, first because it is not clear whether he believed himself to be the equal of Plato and Newton and, in any case, his published works were written for a general audience, not as secret counsel to the powerful. Yet they might be beneficial in a second, more complicated way. For while Rousseau argued that in a virtuous society the sciences and arts should not be encouraged and, perhaps, that they should be suppressed under some circumstances, these recommendations were irrelevant to his age, in which the sciences and arts had already reached peaks that they had not visited since antiquity.

In other words, if the sciences and arts are bad for a good society, it does not follow that they are bad for a bad society as well. On the contrary, Rousseau argued that his society had already succumbed to all of the vices that follow from the development of intellectual culture, so it could hardly be further injured by then. He thought that the price of science and art was a society that is vain, trivial, unequal and tyrannical. Yet his estimation of France at the time is that it exhibited these qualities to the most extreme degree, so it could hardly be injured by his own literary work. And, in fact, he thought that the right kind of art and philosophy might actually improve things. While the sciences and arts are bad for a good society, they could be good for a bad one. He thought there was nothing for him to do except take up the weapons of his enemy and use them for his own ends.

In his reply to Leszinzki, who charged him precisely with this contradiction, he said, 'I might in this connection report what the Church Fathers used to say regarding the worldly Sciences which they despised, and which they nevertheless made use of to combat the Heathen Philosophers. I could cite the comparison they used to draw between these worldly sciences and the jewelry of the Egyptians stolen by the Israelites: but as a final Answer, I will leave it at submitting the following question: If someone came to kill me and I had the good fortune to seize upon his weapon, would I be forbidden to use it to drive him off, before I threw it away?' (D 36). He later made this argument even in defence of *Julie*, a work that had otherwise caused him some discomfort and embarrassment. In his Preface to the novel, he used the common literary device of pretending to be an editor who merely collected the letters of the protagonists, and in this guise wrote, 'There must be theaters in large cities and novels for corrupt peoples. I have observed the morals of my time, and I have published these letters. Would that I had lived in a century when my duty would have been to throw them in the fire' (N 35).

Some readers have questioned either Rousseau's honesty or his self-awareness, arguing that his motivations for writing these works were the same as all the writers whom he criticized. If, in his view, artists and intellectuals are typically vain and self-important, and if they publish mostly to be praised rather than to serve the public, why suppose that he was any different? After all, the 'Discourse' won him immediate praise and some wealth, and *Julie* went on to become unbelievably successful. It would be strange if his works accidentally achieved everything that he excoriated other writers for desiring. Despite his extensive correspondence and autobiographies, there is no reliable way to probe into his motives, which to some degree were probably hidden even to him. So the question of whether he violated his own principles cannot be answered directly. And, in any case, his subjective psychological motivations are irrelevant to the truth or falsehood of his claim that the sciences and arts are good for a bad society.

But to the degree that mere speculation is useful, one can see some truth in his claim that he would rather not have been a philosopher or writer at all. He often said that if his childhood and education had been better, he would have been happy to live quietly as a skilled craftsman and citizen of Geneva. So while it is true that Rousseau the man could not have avoided being a creative genius, it is also true that he sometimes wished he had been someone else. He was conscious of himself as a product of the culture that he criticized, but his criticism of that culture was, in part, that it produced people like him. Of course, he believed that in some ways he was above the mere vanity and duplicity of his time, and that he was more honest than any of his colleagues. But that honesty required him to see that he was an unhappy man and that he had been made that way by his odd education and corrupt surroundings. The laziness and selfishness that he found so distasteful was partly his own, which is why he was so aware of it in others.

This speaks directly to the question of whether the sciences and arts can improve a society that they have already corrupted. Rousseau believed the answer was yes, because they could be used as tools to diagnose and cure the very diseases that they produced.

Romantic literature like *Julie* is a convenient example. He argued that such literature made people vain and trivial. But to people already corrupted by these vices it might have the opposite effect. If he could use all the devices of literature to paint a compelling picture of rustic virtue and a repulsive picture of urban vice, then he might accomplish his goal of using the instruments of high culture against itself. The same is true of the 'Discourse'. He used the tools of polished eloquence and the learned Academy of Dijon to advance a vision of the good life that rejected such eloquence and learned academies.

One may of course doubt whether this project was possible, even in theory. Could supreme thinkers and artists such as Rousseau use the sciences and arts to undermine their own influence? To this there is no clear answer. On the one hand, he seems to have succeeded in a small way in the sense that the obsession with Graeco-Roman civilization that characterized the late eighteenth century in France may be attributed partly to the power of Rousseau's vision of antique virtue. Indeed, the extraordinary reception given to American colonists has been traced to their resemblance (in the French mind) to the heroes of the ancient Roman Republic. There is also endless testimony from people who tried to live out the ideals that he put forward in his major works, people who tried to love like Julie, to raise their children to be like Emile, and to found governments based on his theory of the social contract.

Plus, there is the testimony of Rousseau's own life. The vision of martial virtue that motivated him was in fact his own artistic creation. Based on his reading of Plutarch and his father's stories about great Genevan patriots, he drew his own ideal of a certain kind of virtue, a life of frugality, honesty and self-sacrifice. Beginning in the 1750s he tried to model his life after his own creation, to embody or to live out his own creative vision. He settled down to a steady job as a copyist in order to make his life more like the ideal of virtue that he had created in his imagination. So, to some extent it seems that Rousseau did succeed in using philosophy and art in the service of rustic virtue.

Yet in other ways his success was limited. While he did take steps to bring his character and outward circumstances into line with his idea of antique virtue, he did not take it as far as one might imagine. He was the first to admit that throughout his adult life his character remained far from the Graeco-Roman ideal. While he had moments of great energy, discipline and public spiritedness, he could also be lazy, unfocused and a kind of prudish voluptuary. Something similar might be said of the broader society. While he may have been one of the forces that moved French culture from the baroque and rococo style to the neoclassical, one could not say that French neoclassical civilization resembled Sparta or Rome in the time of the Republic. The leading figures in the age of Louis XV and Louis XVI may have admired ancient heroes such as Leonides and modern pseudo-rustics such as Benjamin Franklin, but they did not resemble them.

One may perhaps gauge their attitudes by looking at the Hameau de la Reine, a rustic retreat built for the queen, Marie Antoinette, on the grounds of the palace at Versailles. The brand new buildings were deliberately made to look like decrepit farmhouses, mills and creameries, although their interiors were elegant and fitted with extraordinary modern conveniences. The queen even installed a single farming family from the countryside to give the hamlet an extra degree of reality. The queen and her retainers could wash the cows, which were specially chosen for their docility, and then milk them into porcelain urns adorned with the queen's monogram. This suggests that by the 1780s Rousseau's ideal of rustic virtue had seeped into the bones of French high culture and also that it had almost no real influence on people's character. If anything, they became more self-absorbed and gloating as the century went on. His experiment of using the weapons of a corrupt culture against itself was not very successful in reforming either his own character or his general society. Of course, some people have interpreted the French Revolution of 1789 as his ultimate vindication.

CONCLUSION

Debate over the meaning and validity of Rousseau's arguments in the 'Discourse' has continued from 1750 until today. In particular, scholars have suggested that the line of causes that he traced in his analysis of cultural decline is ultimately circular. He said that the sciences and arts lead to the corruption of *moeurs*, but he also said that only corrupt societies develop sciences and arts in the first place. Science and art lead to leisure and laziness, but only lazy people with too much leisure engage in them. Science and art make people petty, but only a petty person would be interested in them to begin with. Furthermore, even if he can show that the corruption of society follows the development of the sciences and arts, this does not prove it causes it. The fact that one thing follows another does not prove that the second is caused by the first. A fever sometimes follows a sore throat but it is not caused by the sore throat; both are caused by an underlying infection. Rousseau did not establish clearly that the sciences and arts cause the corruption that he thinks always accompanies them.

He admitted that he was not clear on these issues, yet his logic was stronger than it might seem. On the first objection, he could admit that there may be feedback between two causes, high culture on one side and corrupt *moeurs* on the other. As George Orwell said, 'an effect can become a cause, reinforcing the original cause and producing the same effect in an intensified form, and so on indefinitely. A man may take to drink because he feels himself to be a failure, and then fail all the more completely because he drinks.' The same logic might apply to a culture at large. It might take up the sciences and arts because it is corrupt and become all the more corrupt for having taken them up, which then causes it to take them up further, and so on. Again, Rousseau's argument was not that science and art are the only bad things, but that they are bad things nonetheless, and that they usually make things worse.

Regarding the second objection, he tried to answer it in his reply to Leszinski, who among his many intelligent comments had said that Rousseau was unclear about the order of the links in the chain of causality between intellectual culture and moral decline. Rousseau answered, 'Here is how I would order this genealogy. The first source of evil is inequality; from inequality arose riches . . . From riches are born luxury and idleness; from luxury arose the fine Arts, and from idleness the Sciences' (D 45). This is an interesting twist in the argument because it puts the ultimate blame on inequality rather than the sciences and arts themselves, which are only an intermediate cause between inequalities at one end and vice at the other. This is precisely the thesis that he advanced in his next masterpiece, 'Discourse on the Origin and Foundations of Inequality'.

A further weak point in the essay is his claim that people like Bacon and Newton are vital to a strong society but that a general intellectual culture is bad. His assumption is that the giants of science, philosophy and art spring forth on their own with no help from a wider high culture. Certainly it is common for geniuses, especially in modern times, to stress their individuality and to claim that their teachers only held them back. Machiavelli is a good example as is Descartes, who never tired of criticizing the scholastic philosophy that he studied in his youth. Yet it remains true that Descartes spent his youth in one of the best Jesuit schools in Europe and it is impossible to imagine that he could have achieved his later discoveries in science and philosophy without that training and outside the exciting intellectual atmosphere of northern Europe in the early seventeenth century. Newton was more honest when he admitted that he stood on the shoulders of giants. This raises the question of how such intellectual intensity can be sustained among philosophers and scientists while the majority of the people remain, as Rousseau would have them, in blissful, rustic ignorance. Plato's *Republic* again suggests a possible answer, but not one that Rousseau was likely to defend. And Plato himself was a product of Athens, not of Sparta.

In any case, readers today will probably concentrate on weaknesses in his argument other than those that interested Leszinski and other critics in the eighteenth century. In particular, the modern reader will surely say that Rousseau underestimated the power and value of technology, particularly in the field of medicine. After all, the scientific culture that he criticized has since produced countless benefits to health and welfare. In light of these advances it is hard to agree that life in ancient Sparta or Rome was better than life today, at least in places with access to healthcare. Yet, save infant mortality, people today are not that much healthier than in the ancient world. This was certainly true in Rousseau's epoch. He wrote, 'I shall ask whether there is any solid evidence to conclude that in Countries where this art [medicine] is most neglected man's average life span is shorter than in those where it is cultivated with the greatest care' (D 137). But it is true to a surprising extent today. In Old Testament times the human life span was thought to be 'three score and ten years', or 70, as Psalm 90 says. But things have not improved much in the intervening millennia. The life expectancy of a male born in the United States today is about 74.

Of course this alone does not prove that intellectual culture actually makes life worse. The only evidence for this more radical claim is provided, if at all, by social science combined with intense introspection. The reader must consider what ultimately makes a life fulfilling, and then ask whether the progress of the sciences and arts tends to promote or hinder these things. Yet even if one disagrees with Rousseau's claim that intellectual culture makes people less moral and less happy, one cannot deny that he raised the right question. The only way to tell if human life is getting better or worse is to have a vision of what makes a life good in the first place. Merely to note, as Rousseau's contemporaries did, that some people are becoming richer, and others are becoming more powerful, and still others are gaining greater domination over nature, will not answer the question until one sees how those riches and powers and domination affect the world at large, and until one asks what part (if any) they have in a fulfilled life. Many people will reject Rousseau's own vision of the good life, the life of ancient, martial virtue. But it is impossible to deny his central insight, that the idea of progress is meaningless without a vision of what kind of life is genuinely satisfying, and what kind of society would promote it.

CHAPTER 3

'DISCOURSE ON THE ORIGIN AND FOUNDATIONS OF INEQUALITY'

The years following the publication of his first 'Discourse' were very busy for Rousseau. In addition to responding to critics of that essay, he was briefly but decisively involved in the debate over the relative merits of French and Italian music. In this context he wrote his Italian-style opera *The Village Soothsayer* as well as his controversial 'Letter on French Music' in which he attacked the ideas of Rameau, the most famous composer in France. He also continued to develop his theory of 'the natural goodness of man'. He wrote of this period, 'When my ailments allowed me to go out, and when I was not dragged hither and thither by my acquaintances, I went for solitary walks, during which I reflected on my great system and jotted down some relevant ideas, with the aid of a pocket-book and pencil which I always carried' (C 343). In the middle of all this, in November 1753, the Dijon Academy announced another essay contest. This time the theme would be, 'What is the origin of inequality among men, and is it authorized by the natural law?' Rousseau saw immediately that this topic would allow him to extend his theory in new and important directions. He stopped replying to critics of the first 'Discourse' and began work on a new essay, which he believed would give him 'the opportunity to develop [my principles] in a work of the greatest importance' (C 361).

From the beginning he did not expect or even hope that it would win the prize. He said of his new work that Diderot's 'advice was most useful to me in the writing of it. But nowhere in Europe did it find more than a few readers who understood it, and not one of them chose to speak of it. It had been written to compete for the prize. I sent it in, therefore, though I was certain beforehand that it would not win, for I knew very well that it was not for work of this kind that Academy prizes were founded' (C 362–63). He was right, in a way. The essay had nothing like the immediate impact of his first 'Discourse'. The jury did not even finish reading it because of its length and tone, and although it was published soon afterwards it did not cause the same stir as the earlier essay.

Yet it was a much more profound work, and its influence on subsequent generations was immeasurable. Rousseau knew from the outset that it would provide him with a chance to give full expression to his radical ideas about human life and society, so he took much more care in its composition than he had with the first 'Discourse'. He said, 'I was struck by this great question and surprised at the Academy's daring to propose it. But since they had the courage, I thought that I might be bold enough to discuss it, and set about the task' (C 361–62). One reason that the question perfectly suited his purposes was that his theory of the 'the natural goodness of man', which he had first defended in the previous 'Discourse', raised a glaring question. If people are naturally good, why are they so bad? The first 'Discourse' attributed it, at least in part, to the development of high culture; yet this was not a complete answer. For, if people are naturally good, then either they should never have developed the sciences and arts in the first place, or they should have done good things with them rather than bad. This is the underlying paradox of Rousseau's philosophy. 'Men are wicked; a sad and constant experience makes proof unnecessary; yet man is naturally good, I believed I have proved it; what, then, can have depraved him to this point?' (D 197). The second 'Discourse' set out to solve the paradox.

BACKGROUND

As with Rousseau's first 'Discourse', the reader today needs some background to understand the Academy's question and how Rousseau shaped it to his purposes. The first issue is that the term 'inequality' was not limited to economics, as one might think. Certainly one of the obvious kinds of inequality in Rousseau's milieu was the economic disparity of pre-revolutionary France. Yet this was not the only or even the most important kind of inequality relevant to the Academy's question. In the years before the revolution, French society still showed remnants of its feudal past; in particular its citizens were divided into various social and legal categories, each of which had its own rights and responsibilities. The most general categories were the three 'Estates', the clergy, the nobility and the commoners. But in fact things were more complicated than that, because land ownership brought certain rights and duties that blurred the Estates; and within the Third Estate the wealthy urban population tended to dominate, leaving the peasants on their own. Furthermore, the inequalities between men and women operated within and between the Estates in many subtle ways. The result was a highly complicated and stratified society.

Economic status was a further dimension of inequality, yet it did not match perfectly with the hierarchy of the Estates, because by Rousseau's time some of the wealthiest people in France (such as his friend and sometime employer Claude Dupin, the owner of the chateau at Chenonceau) were descended from country squires rather than from the high nobility, and had acquired their wealth through manufacturing or the civil service. The ideas and attitudes embedded in such a society are difficult to recapture from the perspective of a modern liberal democracy. Today, even the people who are least worried about the inequalities in present society tend to assume that all people are 'created equal' in some meaningful sense, which implies that existing inequalities are due to luck, or character, or some such contingent factors, rather than being permanently built into the nature of things.

The meaning of *égalité* in the revolutionary slogan, '*Liberté, égalité, fraternité*' was precisely that every citizen should start out with the same rights and duties. Article Six of the 'Declaration of the Rights of Man and of the Citizen', written during the Revolution in 1789, stated 'All citizens, being equal in the eyes of the law, are equally eligible to all dignities and to all public positions and occupations, according to their abilities, and without distinction except that of their virtues and talents'. It is a principle that underlies most modern democracies, as least in theory if not in fact. Thus when Rousseau turned to the question of the origin of inequality, he had in mind all the complicated and overlapping inequalities that defined French society, not merely their economic dimension. He said that this kind of inequality 'consists in the different privileges which some men enjoy to the prejudice of the others, such as to be more wealthy, more honored, more Powerful than they, or even to get themselves obeyed by them' (D131). In particular, he interpreted the Academy's question in terms of political power rather than merely money.

The Academy's question contains a second difficulty for the modern reader, this one concerning the phrase 'natural law'. This term had been used through the history of social and political philosophy at least from the time of the Stoics in ancient Greece and Rome, and it has been given dozens of different interpretations. The Academy did not specify which if any it had in mind, and Rousseau complained at the beginning of the 'Discourse' that the term has been used in so many ways as to make it almost useless. 'Among the most serious Writers, scarcely two can be found who are of the same opinion on this point. To say nothing of the Ancient Philosophers who seem deliberately to have set out to contradict one another on the most fundamental principles' (D 126). Nonetheless, there is a common root idea of natural law, which is that there are moral rules for human conduct that exist somehow over and above the traditions and written laws of individual societies. They are moral laws that are built into the structure of things, as opposed to those that exist merely by human convention. Philosophers have disagreed over what these laws are, where they come from, how they can be known, and what makes them morally binding. Yet beneath these differences there is a belief that rules of human conduct and political organization are somehow sewn into the fabric of reality.

The most prominent version of the natural law theory holds that there are certain goals or ends that are appropriate to all human beings, and that people can discover the rules for achieving these ends; these rules in turn are 'natural laws' in the sense that they describe principles for how people should act in order to reach their natural ends. For example, most natural law philosophers (although not Rousseau) have argued that it is part of human nature to be social; people, like ants and bees, naturally live in groups. This means that the preservation of society is an end that is built into human nature. And since the preservation of society requires, among other things, respect for property rights, one can say that there are natural laws that state 'Don't steal' and 'Give back what you have borrowed'. Again, there was much debate about the appropriate goals of human life, about how we can know them, and about what makes it obligatory to promote them in ourselves and in others. Yet there remains the idea that by studying human nature one can discover moral laws of individual and social behaviour.

In the centuries after Rousseau, the idea of natural law has come under attack from two different and powerful directions. One idea, associated with the Romantic movement and later with existentialism, was that there is no such thing as human nature or, if there is, we cannot know it. The less radical version of this view was expressed in the closing lines of William Wordsworth's 'The Tables Turned'. 'Sweet is the lore which Nature brings;/Our meddling intellect/Misshapes the beauteous forms of things–/We murder to dissect./Enough of Science and of Art,/Close up those barren leaves;/Come forth, and bring with you a heart/That watches and receives'. On this view, human nature can be known (if it can be known at all) only through a personal, existential experience rather than through philosophical analysis. Thus there is little possibility of a moral science or an objective, universal natural law. The more radical version of this theory denies that there is such a thing as human nature in the first place. A number of thinkers, from Søren Kierkegaard to Michel Foucault, have argued that there is no single nature that lies beneath various historical contingencies and social constructions. They have claimed (speaking generally) that all of the basic categories in which philosophers have tried to capture human life are projections or constructions of the will rather than some kind of objective analysis of what it is to be human. From this perspective, the idea of a natural law appears to be nothing but an arbitrary instrument to constrain the diversity and ambiguity of life.

The second major line of attack on the philosophy of natural law descends from Rousseau's contemporary David Hume, who argued that even if there is such a thing as human nature, and even if we can know what it is, it does not follow that it is good to fulfil or promote it, or that we are morally obligated to do so. Hume thus inaugurated what has come to be called 'the fact-value distinction' in moral philosophy, according to which no list of facts about the world can, by itself, define what is good or obligatory. For example, it may be true that humans are naturally social, but how does it follow that one ought to do things that preserve society and not to do things that harm society? It follows only on the assumption that what is natural is good and a source of moral obligations, but this is nowhere implied in the mere claim that people are naturally social. What makes something valuable, according to Hume, is simply that we care about it, and this is extrinsic to the act or object itself. Thus, saying that an action or person is morally good has the same logic as saying that a piece of food tastes good. It is a report on how one feels about something rather than a statement about its inherent qualities. This was Hume's point in saying, 'Morality, therefore, is more properly felt than judg'd of'.

The power of these objections caused a decline of natural law philosophies in the nineteenth and twentieth centuries, yet the theory has continued to make progress, especially among Catholic philosophers. Rousseau's place in the natural law tradition is highly ambiguous for reasons discussed below and in the next chapter. Yet, in writing his second 'Discourse', he accepted the general method of that tradition. He began with an analysis of human nature, from which he attempted to discover what kind of life and what sort of moral rules are appropriate to such a being. Yet even at the surface there is a difference between Rousseau's idea of natural law and that of his predecessors. For he proposed an evolutionary account of humanity, according to which human nature changes depending on environmental and social conditions. This makes his idea of natural law more complicated than others in that tradition and, indeed, it may place him outside that tradition entirely, especially as he went on to deny that humans are necessarily social. In any case, the idea that the natural law cannot be defined independently of the individual's environment is the great point of originality in his account. It is the insight that most influenced later generations and made his second 'Discourse' such a revolutionary work.

A final difficulty with respect to the Academy's question is that, once again, Rousseau changed the wording to fit his own ideas and purposes. The Academy had asked about the origin of inequality and whether it is justified by natural law. Rousseau used the opening provided by the word 'origin' to write an entire speculative history of human social institutions, and then mostly dropped the idea of natural law from his presentation. He changed his title to the more ambiguous 'Discourse on the Origin and Foundations of Inequality', and under this label advanced an extraordinary theory of human nature and the justification of social institutions. The question that Rousseau really asked and answered was: why are there people of different political, social and economic ranks, and are these inequalities justifiable morally? In answering this question he further refined his theory of 'the natural goodness of man'.

THE ARGUMENT

The debate over inequality, over why some people should have more authority and advantages than others, was one of the central questions of political philosophy in the seventeenth and eighteenth centuries. Thus, perhaps the easiest way to approach Rousseau's very original answer is to see how it was different from what his readers might have expected. The traditional argument for the origin of inequality was that it came from God in the sense that monarchs and other rulers had a 'divine right' to their authority over their subjects. A classic text from Proverbs states, 'By me kings reign, and princes decree justice. By me princes rule, and nobles, even all the judges of the earth', and many people took this passage at face value. It was the argument put forward by Robert Filmer in England and Jacques-Bénigne Bossuet in France, to name only the most influential sources. To a reader today, the 'divine right' theory of political authority may seem weak, but philosophers at the time developed it in many interesting and profound ways.

One version of this theory argued that political power comes to secular authorities from God through the pope. This view was quite logical and occasionally influential. If the pope is God's vice-regent on earth, as some believed, then he must have authority to appoint subsidiary rulers over various nations, much as, for example, the mayor of a city might have the authority to appoint someone to oversee the city's parks. On this theory kings and queens, emperors and empresses, are territorial governors appointed by the pope, who in turn receives his power from God. This theory of political authority, which has remarkable clarity and simplicity, influenced European thought and political history in many ways.

The most obvious was when, in 800, Pope Leo III crowned Charlemagne emperor of the Romans. While it was done for selfish reasons and was perhaps without significant precedent, it showed at least that a pope might feel qualified to crown an emperor. Similarly, in the fifteenth century, when the kingdoms of Spain and Portugal found themselves in territorial disputes over their claims in Africa and the Americas, they appealed to the pope for a resolution. The underlying idea was that since he is God's representative, he should decide who gets what. In this case, because little was known about the geography of South America, the pope's decision was not as equitable as it might have been, which explains why Portuguese is spoken in Brazil but the rest of South and Central America speaks Spanish. Echoes of these traditions were heard even into the nineteenth century, for example when Napoleon had the pope bless his crown during his coronation as Emperor of the French.

Yet the idea that political authority comes to secular leaders from God through the pope was destined to have more detractors than defenders even in Catholic countries. Among its greatest enemies were, of course, the various monarchs who did not care to think of themselves as provincial governors under a sovereign papacy. This tension showed itself in the series of religious controversies that pervaded European politics from the medieval period onwards. One question was whether the pope had the authority to remove temporal rulers and replace them with those of his choosing, which on the strict interpretation of this theory he should have. Yet there were few rulers and few of their subjects who would grant that authority to him, and few times that the pope had power to enforce his will. What the popes did retain was the power to excommunicate, which they exercised regularly, most obviously in the case of Henry VIII in England.

There were also related controversies about whether monarchs had the authority to punish clerics who broke the civil law and whether it was the pope or the temporal ruler who had the power to choose church leadership and receive income from religious establishments. These were more prolonged and difficult struggles, especially in France. They were answered decisively on the side of the temporal rulers only when, under the reign of Louis XIV, the 'Declaration of the Clergy of France' stated, 'St Peter and the popes, his successors, and the Church itself have dominion from God only over things spiritual and not over things temporal and civil. Therefore kings and sovereigns are not beholden to the church in deciding temporal things. They cannot be deposed by the church and their subjects cannot be absolved by the church from their oaths of allegiance.'

Furthermore, this theory of political authority was moot in Protestant countries that rejected the claims of the bishop of Rome to be head of the Church and God's vice-regent on earth. Yet a number of influential philosophers developed theories of 'divine right' that did not rely on the pope to be an intermediary between God and temporal rulers. The Protestant King James I of England, in a speech to Parliament, said, 'The State of monarchy is the supremest thing upon earth: for kings are not only God's lieutenants upon earth, and sit upon God's throne, but even by God himself they are called Gods.' This was a way of affirming the majesty of the monarch without referring to the pope. The cruder version of this argument, perhaps, was the one proposed by Filmer, who argued that monarchs have political authority because they are (literally or figuratively) the parents of their subjects, and ultimately receive their title from the first parent of all, Adam, and thus from Noah who was the patriarch of the only family supposed to have survived the biblical flood. In his work *Patriarcha*, Filmer said, 'It may seem absurd to maintain that kings now are the fathers of their people, since experience shows the contrary. It is true, all kings be not the natural parents of their subjects, yet they all either are, or are to be reputed as the next heirs to those progenitors who were at first the natural parents of the whole people, and in their right succeed to the exercise of supreme jurisdiction. And such heirs are not only lords of their own children, but also of their brethren, and all others that were subject to their fathers.'

The plausibility of this view, if there was any, came from the passages in Genesis that show God giving the earth and all its creatures to Adam. Filmer tried to argue that the authority which Adam held over the natural world, as well as over Eve and their children, had descended in a lineal way to present-day political rulers. The attraction of this theory was that it made the monarch's authority over his or her subjects a subset of the power that parents have over children, which conveniently left the pope out of it. Yet the weaknesses of the theory were debilitating, as Locke demonstrated with great apparent pleasure, in his *First Treatise of Government*. Filmer's argument did nothing to explain why, after millennia of usurpations and civil wars, one particular living adult in the present should have authority over another, which is what a theory of sovereignty is supposed to do in the first place.

Yet there were also a number of sophisticated Protestant theories of 'divine right', one of the most telling of which was developed by Luther himself and then extended in interesting ways by philosophers like Hobbes. Luther argued that humans are inherently sinful and incapable of doing good things on their own without, and perhaps even with, God's grace. The upshot is that the world is full of people who, because they are inherently and irredeemably corrupt, will sin continually and in doing so cause great harm to one another. The purpose of political authority on this view is, as much as possible, to prevent people from harming one another, or to make earthly life as bearable as it can be even though it will continue to be quite miserable. This is why Luther called political authority a 'divine institution' – not because he thought political power came from God to earthly rulers in a direct way, but because God created a world that requires strong temporal authority to keep the peace.

So Luther too believed that monarchs rule by 'divine right', but in the limited sense that earthly authority, of any kind, furthers the divine purposes of preventing people from harming one another. As one would expect, Luther had scripture to defend his view, especially Paul's letter to the Romans, which states, 'Let every soul be subject unto the higher powers. For there is no power but of God: the powers that be are ordained of God. Whosoever therefore resisteth the power, resisteth the ordinance of God: and they that resist shall receive to themselves damnation.' From this he drew the conclusion that it is always wrong to revolt against political authority. Even if one is ordered to sin, he said, it is wrong to revolt; all one can do is refuse to sin and then accept the punishments meted out by the temporal authority.

Divine right was, however, only one of the traditional theories of the origin of inequality. Aristotle provided another. He argued that some people are suited to rule, and should rule, just by virtue of their nature or character, independent of a supernatural sanction. While his political theory is very complicated, it is based on the idea that some people, because of their intelligence and other qualities, are natural rulers and should have the rest of humanity under their supervision. On this view, it is not God who gives one person a right to rule; rather it is that person's own ability to organize things for the best that confers that right. His theory seems strange to some modern readers, so perhaps an analogy will help. One can imagine a farm and all the creatures that inhabit it, from the trees in the woodland, to the crops in the field, to the livestock, to the pets, to the children, to the farmer. If one then asks which one of all these creatures should run the farm, or which one should rule, the answer is obvious. The farmer should rule, because he or she is the one who knows how to organize things for the best of everyone else.

Aristotle's view of politics was similar to this. The ruler should be the person who knows how to organize things for the good of everyone and has the skill to make it happen; and in turn this knowledge and skill gives that superior person the right to tell others what to do and to expect obedience. This theory denies, obviously, that all people are 'created equal', a fact which has kept his political views out of the mainstream of debate in most modern democratic societies. Indeed, he argued that some people are 'natural slaves' who should not be allowed to participate as equals in public life, and he also believed that women are inferior to men in a way that disqualified them from citizenship. It is impossible to find space for such views within the set of concepts that frame debate in modern democratic societies, such as universal suffrage, individual liberty and equality before the law. Even in Rousseau's time, Aristotle's ideas were not especially popular, at least in their pure form, perhaps because they might require rulers to demonstrate their superior intellect and character.

In any case, Rousseau rejected both theories of the origin of inequality. He denied that God gives anyone a special right to rule others, and he also denied that a mere superiority of strength or intellect gives one moral authority to tell others what to do and to be obeyed. The core of Rousseau's argument was that inequality is a human construction and nothing more. If some people have the power to rule and if others feel compelled to submit, it is so only because the contingencies of history have produced such institutions and formed the kind of people who inhabit them. He went on to argue, in his second 'Discourse' and more fully in *The Social Contract*, that some of these artificial constructions are better than others, or that some structures of power are more justifiable than others. But all of them, he said, are the result of human convention. One of the revolutionary aspects of his 'Discourse' was its argument that the structures of power and obedience that people created in his own milieu, eighteenth-century France, were unjustifiable. He claimed, albeit indirectly, that they were the products of historical accident and fraud, rather than of nature or God's purpose. One can easily imagine how stunning his argument must have seemed to those who read it carefully in the France of Louis XV, when they found that, on Rousseau's view, the monarch of the great nation held his throne neither by divine sanction, nor by virtue of his superior merit, but rather because of chance and usurpation.

He presented his theory of the origin of inequality through the device of the 'state of nature', and this part of his theory can be somewhat confusing. The concept of the 'state of nature' pervaded the political thought of the period but, like 'natural law', it meant different things to different people. For Rousseau, it referred to the state of affairs that would exist if human beings were stripped of artificial qualities, or qualities that they could possess only from being members of an existing society. The inhabitants of the state of nature are people who lack the conventional or artificial character traits that come only from belonging to a certain social group. Thus, the state of nature was simply a device for interpreting and depicting the elements of human nature. He chose this method of presentation not only because it was a standard device among political theorists of his time, but also because it allowed him to argue that inequality comes into being at a particular, contingent moment. Rousseau explained the origin of inequality by means of a theory of how humanity moved (or might have moved) from the state of nature, where there was no inequality, to the present arrangement of things where inequality is pervasive.

He said that to know the origin of inequality we must begin 'by knowing men themselves', implying that he intended to look at humanity, 'as Nature formed him, through all the changes which the succession of times and of things must have wrought in his original constitution, and disentangle what he owes to his own stock from what circumstances and his progress have added to or changed from his primitive state' (D 124). The story he went on to tell is well known and fairly easy to follow in his text, so there is no reason to trace all the details here. Speaking generally, in the original condition, which he sometimes called the 'pure state of nature', human beings lived an extraordinarily simple outward life and were governed by very simple psychological traits. 'I see an animal less strong than some, less agile than others, but, all things considered, the most advantageously organized of all: I see him sating his hunger beneath an oak, slaking his thirst at the first Stream, finding his bed at the foot of the same tree that supplied his meal, and with that his needs are satisfied' (D 134).

He further argued that, in the original condition, nature was abundant and people had few needs and wants. In fact, they had only two basic drives, which were an instinct for self-preservation and a tendency to feel pain at the suffering of others. People would also have possessed a latent capacity for free will and the trait of 'perfectibility' or the capacity to learn new things over a lifetime and from one generation to the next (D 140–42). The result was a state in which people felt satisfied and self-reliant. He said that, 'since the state of Nature is the state in which the care for our own preservation is the least prejudicial to the self-preservation of others, it follows that this state was the most conducive to Peace and the best suited to Mankind' (D 151). He depicted them as, 'wandering in the forests without industry, without speech, without settled abode, without war, and without tie, without any need of others of his kind and without any desire to harm them. . . . subject to few passions and self-sufficient' (D 157).

While this theory of a peaceful and equal state of nature is the most famous part of his second 'Discourse' it is not the whole story, because he went on, in Part II, to explain how inequality might have come into being among creatures that were originally benign and scattered. The most important part of the scenario is that as the human population grew it spread out into less fruitful climates, the result of which was that people encountered scarcity and must have begun to live in groups in order to survive (D 162). This had the dual effect of bringing people into more regular acquaintance with one another and of enlarging their intellectual capacities. In these circumstances, people began to develop comparative notions such as great and small, strong and weak, and they eventually realized that others were judging them just as they judged others (D 165–66). At this moment there arose a desire to be regarded highly by one's peers.

To express this idea of 'wanting to be envied' Rousseau used the term *amour-propre*, which is an essential but complicated concept in his work. At the risk of simplifying too much, it is a socialized form of the natural human concern for one's own well-being, and might best be translated as 'vanity' (D 218, 377). To explain the idea he imagined a scenario that might have taken place once people had begun to interact more regularly. 'Everyone began to look at everyone else and to wish to be looked at himself, and public esteem acquired a price. The one who sang or danced the best; the handsomest, the strongest, the most skillful, or the most eloquent, came to be the most highly regarded' (D 166). To put it succinctly, vanity is the desire to be regarded as better than other people and, in this sense, it is a desire not for a determinate good like food or shelter, but rather for a kind of relative consideration, and this is the source of inequality. 'If one sees a handful of powerful and rich men at the pinnacle of greatness and fortune while the masses grovel in obscurity and misery, it is because the former value the things they enjoy only to the extent that the others are deprived of them, and they would cease to be happy if, without any change in their own state, the People ceased to be miserable' (D 184).

The idea that people desire to possess things and to have power mostly in order to make others feel envious is the most characteristic aspect of Rousseau's social theory and the foundation of his account of inequality. Perhaps a further example will bring out his point more fully. Many people desire to possess an expensive automobile. Now, it is one thing to desire to go from one place to another, which is a basic need that is somewhat independent of society; but it is another to desire a luxurious car. The difference is that the standard for luxury is relative to one's society and the desire to reach that standard is shaped by society, because in different circumstances the same person would often wish to reach a different standard. Luxurious automobiles are considered luxurious not because of their intrinsic qualities, but because they are more sumptuous than those of one's peers, whoever they happen to be; and the desire to possess one is not a desire for transportation, but rather a desire to be envied. When everyone else walks, the person who has a small car feels very pleased; but that car becomes undesirable as soon as everyone else has one like it, even though the vehicle itself has not changed. Rousseau argued that such is the case with most things that people desire and especially with money itself and political power.

The idea that many social institutions are based on vanity was not unique to Rousseau. Hobbes, for example, had made a large place in his political theory for 'honour' or the desire to be viewed as superior to others. And even the classical economists of Rousseau's time had begun to see the importance of vanity in economic institutions. One scholar has noted in this connection that Rousseau's contemporary, Adam Smith, had developed the argument 'that if people were ruled by economic motives alone, there would be little stimulus to increase production above necessities and needs. It is because men are driven by an impulse for status that economic "development" began'. Rousseau's contribution was to say that economic development generally makes people even more vain, which in turn causes them to wish even more that their peers do badly. It causes them to be envious of more advantaged people and scornful of less advantaged, all while feeling unhappy with their own state. This is another facet of his overall insight, that many of the things that people regard as progress, such as scientific and economic development, actually make people less happy and less virtuous than they would have been without them.

In sum, Rousseau argued that the origin of inequality was neither God nor nature, but simple human vanity. Because people desire to be envied, they find it necessary to create political, social and economic institutions that allow them to demonstrate their superiority over others. If a few people are powerful, and others are famous, and still others are rich, while the masses are oppressed, reviled and poor, it is because people have constructed institutions that have no other source and purpose than to allow the few to feel superior to the many. This outlook gave him unique and powerful tools for explaining institutions like money and even government itself. His view on private property is especially interesting, because he saw it as a trick played by the clever and powerful on the dim and weak. 'The first man who, having enclosed a piece of ground, to whom it occurred to say *this is mine*, and found people sufficiently simple to believe him, was the true founder of civil society. How many crimes, wars, murders, how many miseries and horrors Mankind would have been spared by him who, pulling up the stakes or filling in the ditch, had cried out to his kind: Beware of listening to this impostor; You are lost if you forget that the fruits are everyone's and the Earth is no one's' (D 161). He argued that even government itself was a trick by which the powerful compelled others to do their bidding by law and principle rather than by the less efficient means of mere personal force (D 172f).

The details of Rousseau's theory are immensely rich and repay close reading. He offered a theory of reciprocal causality between individuals and their environment, between nature and culture, which showed individuals changing as their society changes and the society changing as its members change, all in a complicated causal relationship with climate, agriculture and the material world generally. It is no wonder that Emile Durkheim viewed Rousseau as one of the founders of sociology. One can imagine the shock that Rousseau's readers must have felt, especially those in the privileged classes, when they read a theory which told them that all of the hierarchies of Church, state and society were the result of human vanity, trickery and stupidity, and that their position had no other legitimacy than that the mass of humanity was too ignorant and too entranced to demolish it.

THE RESPONSE

It is no surprise that Rousseau's audience was upset by his 'Discourse', the only wonder being that he did not face greater challenge and persecution. He himself knew that the work was likely to provoke anger in France and so, after writing it, he immediately left for Geneva, waiting until he crossed the border into the Duchy of Savoy before signing the dedicatory letter at the beginning of the work. The fact that he dedicated the 'Discourse' to the city of Geneva was itself very strange, and it caused him some trouble when he finally reached the place of his birth because even the residents of this semi-democratic city could hardly avoid the charges he levelled against the rich and powerful. Part of the reason that the essay did not cause him more trouble was that it is quite long and difficult to understand compared to his first 'Discourse' and 'Letter Concerning French Music'. In particular, Rousseau attached a series of long and complicated footnotes to the published version that have been a source of confusion and scholarly controversy ever since. The most famous response to the 'Discourse' was Voltaire's caustic remark, 'I have received, Monsieur, your new book against the human race, and I thank you. No one has employed so much intelligence to turn us men into beasts. One starts wanting to walk on all fours after reading your book' (J 306).

Yet the entire meaning of the 'Discourse' turns on the answer to a question that was not much discussed in Rousseau's own time, but which has come to dominate the later interpretation of this great work. He presented a developmental and, it appears, chronological account of the origin of inequality, yet he offered almost no evidence that things happened as he said they did. The sciences of anthropology and archaeology were hardly in their infancy, and the only evidence that he can provide about humanity's prehistory comes from travellers' tales about primitive tribes and orang-utans. This is hardly sufficient evidence for explaining how the social world came to be as it is. Faced with this obvious and insurmountable objection, some scholars have argued that Rousseau never intended his essay to be an account of what actually happened in the prehistory of humanity. But if this is so, it is hard to see how the essay can pretend to explain the origin of inequality. This question requires detailed examination.

On the surface, Rousseau's argument is ambiguous. In some places he suggested that it is a straightforward theory of human history and prehistory, of the historical origins of current social and political institutions. For example, at the beginning of the 'Discourse' he describes his goals in a way that seems unambiguously historical.

He says that he intends to look at man, 'as Nature formed him, through all the changes which the succession of times and of things must have wrought in his original constitution, and to disentangle what he owes to his own stock from what circumstances and his progress have added to or changed in his primitive state' (D 124). Yet soon afterwards he describes the argument as if it were purely hypothetical, with no connection to actual human history. 'For it is no light undertaking to disentangle what is original from what is artificial in man's present Nature, and to know accurately a state which no longer exists, which perhaps never did exist, which probably never will exist' (D 125). He then says, 'Let us therefore begin by setting aside all the facts, for they do not affect the question. The Inquiries that may be pursued regarding this Subject ought not to be taken for historical truths, but only for hypothetical and conditional reasonings; better suited to elucidate the Nature of things than to show their genuine origin' (D 132).

The reader is left to wonder what the place of history is in the essay, and what the theory is a theory of. It seems that if the 'Discourse' was intended to be historical then he tried for some reason to conceal it or, if it was not historical, then he had other ideas about what it means to show 'the origin and foundations' of something. Those who believe that he did intend to offer a theory about real human history must answer the question of why he so often said that he did not. And those who believe he did not intend to offer such a theory must explain what he was talking about instead. For those in the first camp, there is a ready explanation for why he might have tried to conceal his intentions, namely that he feared religious persecution. If Rousseau had been explicit about his historical intentions then, because his theory is incompatible with the Bible, he would have put himself at risk of censorship or other punishment. Indeed, one of Rousseau's own comments hinted in this direction, albeit obliquely. 'Religion commands us to believe that since God Himself drew Men out of the state of Nature immediately after the creation, they are unequal because he wanted them to be so; but it does not forbid us to form conjectures . . . about what Mankind might have become if it had remained abandoned to itself' (D 132).

This interpretation is not implausible and has the virtue of showing how Rousseau's state of nature can have explanatory power. The facts one is to 'set aside' are the biblical facts; and one is to do so in order to clear the way for the real facts, the historical facts. If the argument was intended as history, however, one must admit that it is not very persuasive, because he offered almost no evidence of what human prehistory was actually like. Furthermore, if this interpretation is correct, then Rousseau faces a second and even more damaging objection. His argument seems to lean on the false assumption that, as one critic has put it, 'for any natural species there is (or, but for man's interference, would be) some natural environment and some set of instinctive behavior patterns such is that if a number of members of the species were placed in that environment they would, unless artificially inhibited, adopt the instinctive behavior-patterns and, as a result, live and multiply successfully'.

This assumption is false, according to this objection, because many animals, including human beings, acquire only in social life the knowledge and skills that allow them to survive and multiply in their environment, and that thus define their nature. Certain creatures, if 'abandoned to themselves', would not flourish; they would die, or at least they would have lives that are unnatural for that species, which is to say that they would not exhibit their nature or essence, because part of their essence is to be social. For example, an entomologist who studied what ants do when they are not part of a colony would discover little or nothing about the nature of ants, because part of that nature is to be a member of a colony. Presumably this is also the case with humans. To imagine a human being who has not had a social life, to imagine in particular a human being whose capacity for language has not been developed, would be to imagine something that is not really a human being. The consequence is that Rousseau's state of nature fails as a historical theory. This objection is exceptionally powerful on the assumption that Rousseau intended his theory of the state of nature to describe historical reality. The reasons to accept it, even though it requires one to dismiss many of Rousseau's most adamant claims, are that sometimes Rousseau himself suggested that his work was historical, and that otherwise the state of nature seems to have no explanatory value.

The alternative interpretation is that the state of nature is purely hypothetical or, as one scholar has put it, 'However compelling one may find Rousseau's conjectures in Part I of the *Discourse*, they remain conjectures. He knew that they are conjectures; he said that they are conjectures; and he very clearly spelled out the reasons why they necessarily are conjectures quite independently of the biblical account.' On this reading, when Rousseau said that he would explain the origin of inequality among men, one should not assume that by 'origin' he meant historical development, and 'men' to mean Frenchmen, Englishmen and the like. Instead, Rousseau took aspects of the human character as it does exist in fact and abstracted them from their concrete reality. Of all the features that human beings do or could possess, he took the desire for self-preservation, the capacity to feel pity, perfectibility and the potential for free will. He then removed them from their particulars and assembled them into a simplified, purified being that he called 'natural man', who never (or perhaps never) appeared in nature. On this reading, the fact that this person could not be real is irrelevant, because it was intended to embody a principle, not to be a fact.

In general, the 'hypothetical' interpretation is preferable to the 'historical'. It can account for more of the text because Rousseau himself often said that his work was hypothetical not historical. And while one must grant that there are a number of ambiguous passages, every time that Rousseau was explicit about his intentions, he clearly said that they were hypothetical (D 125, 128, 132, 134). At the end of Part I of the 'Discourse' he said, 'I admit that since the events I have to describe could have occurred in several ways, I can choose between them only on the basis of conjecture; but not only do such conjectures become reasons when they are the most probable that can be derived from the nature of things and the only means available to discover the truth, it also does not follow that the consequences I want to deduce from mine will therefore be conjectural' (D159). This interpretation does, however, raise the problem that the historical one avoided. How can a hypothetical state of nature explain the origin of real inequality?

This is the essential and most difficult interpretative question about the second 'Discourse' and perhaps it has never been answered definitively. But Rousseau's own comments suggest a solution. To understand his point in saying that the events he described 'could have occurred in many ways' and that they are built on 'the basis of conjecture', one can think of an analogy taken from the physical sciences. If a physicist looked at billiard balls dispersed on a table and asked how they came to be that way, there would be many possible answers. One could trace back in time any number of hypothetical collisions that would leave that particular arrangement of balls. So, any theory would be hypothetical in the sense that it would describe one of many possible ways that things could have come to be as they are. Furthermore, in creating the theory, the physicists would refer to many ideal entities, such as a 'frictionless surface' and a 'straight line' and an 'elastic collision' that never exist in reality. Rousseau's state of nature was very much like the physicist's realm of ideal entities and interactions. It is an abstraction, which could never exist as such, but which helps to explain what does exist.

This interpretation is strengthened when one remembers that the second 'Discourse' was concerned not only with the origin of inequality, but also with the question of whether it is justified by natural law. While Rousseau's views on natural law are hard to understand, he unquestionably rejected the idea that natural law can be established by a mere survey of present empirical facts. This was the core of his argument against the philosopher Hugo Grotius and others in that intellectual tradition (D 126–27). Grotius was a natural law theorist who set out to discover whether there are any laws of morality that derive from nature itself, or whether all morality is relative to culture and convention. In doing so he distinguished between two ways of discovering the natural law, which he called the *a priori* and *a posteriori* methods. The *a priori* method, which he regarded as more philosophical but less useful, is the one mentioned above. It deduces the natural law, or the principles of correct action, from the features of human nature. So, for example, he argued that because being alive is necessary for all other goods, it is a natural law that one ought to preserve one's life and that one may use force to defend oneself from unprovoked aggression. The *a posteriori* method, on the other hand, which he said is less certain but more far-reaching, discovers the natural law by looking at what principles most people or most nations accept, even if one is unable to deduce them directly from human nature.

Rousseau argued that the *a posteriori* method, which makes inferences from fact to law, is absurd for reasons expressed in the epigraph of the 'Discourse', which is a passage from Aristotle. 'What is natural has to be investigated not in beings that are depraved, but in those that are good according to nature' (D 113). In other words, one should not use the *a posteriori* method to discover the natural law, because people as they are found in reality today are mostly corrupt, so what is common among them is a poor guide to what is good or right. In other words, one must know what a healthy human being is in order to infer what is good for it, for the rules appropriate to a sick person can be harmful to a healthy one. Furthermore, the knowledge of what is appropriate to a healthy person must necessarily be based on conjecture, because the idea of a 'healthy person' is itself conjectural or hypothetical given that every actual person is ill in one way or another. Rousseau feared that the method of Grotius would justify under the term natural law all the abuses of corrupt governments. 'One could use a more consistent method', he said, 'but not one more favorable to Tyrants' (S 42).

This explains why, in order to answer the question proposed by the Academy, he thought that one must begin, 'by knowing men themselves', and why it is necessary to have 'precise notions' of the original condition 'in order accurately to judge of our present state' (D 125). The reason was that natural law can be deduced only from the knowledge of correctly purified human nature, which means that the danger is not that one will misunderstand the facts but that one will misunderstand the law. 'But so long as we do not know natural man, we shall in vain try to ascertain either the Law which he has received or that which best suits his constitution' (D 127). On this interpretation, the topic of the 'Discourse' is not human history but human nature, which never exists simply as such. The goal of the essay was to show in what sense inequality is a consequence of the principles of human nature and thus to show whether it is a perfection or a corruption of that nature.

Rousseau's goals and method are clear on this reading, yet they do leave a serious question. If his theory was not about human history but rather about abstract human nature, what counts as evidence for or against his views? On the historical interpretation, at least, it would be clear what makes a given theory better or worse than another. One would look for data from, for example, archaeological findings and anthropological studies. But Rousseau's theory is not like this because he meant to defend a view about human nature in general, not just the lives of particular people at a particular time in the past. The answer is that his method, if it can be called that, was introspective. He tried to discover what is essential in human nature by looking within himself. When he first read the announcement for the essay competition he retreated to the countryside to reflect on his answer. He went to the forest and there, 'I sought and I found the vision of those primitive times, the history of which I proudly traced. I demolished the petty lies of mankind; I dared to strip man's nature naked, to follow the progress of time, and trace the things which have distorted it; and by comparing man as he had made himself with man as he is by nature I showed him in his pretended perfection the true source of his misery' (C 362). The reader will have to judge whether such evidence is plausible and sufficient.

One last feature of his argument is worth mentioning. Rousseau has often been credited or charged with defending the thesis of the 'noble savage', or the idea that people living in primitive societies are morally superior to those in more advanced ones. This interpretation is not entirely wrong, yet it needs significant qualification. Although the phrase 'noble savage' appeared nowhere in his work, he undeniably believed that art, science and technology bring out the worst features in people; the thesis of his first 'Discourse' was that high culture tends to make people lazy, vain and duplicitous. The second 'Discourse' extended this argument by showing, in a much richer way, how people might have come to be as corrupt as they are in modern civilizations even on the assumption that they are naturally good. But the issue is complicated, because the two works provided two different ideals against which to measure the corruption of modern society. In the first 'Discourse', the softness and selfishness of the present were contrasted with the virtues of ancient Greece and Rome, whereas in the second Rousseau juxtaposed exploitation in the real world with the egalitarianism of a hypothetical state of nature. This makes the question of the 'noble savage' very complex.

If Rousseau thought that the citizens of Sparta and the Roman Republic were the ideal human type, he could not have been much in favour of 'natural man' or the 'noble savage', because the patriotism and self-sacrifice that characterize antique virtue are completely absent from his description of the state of nature in Part I of the second 'Discourse'. The most that one can say about the state of nature is that it is benign, meaning that the people he described have no interest in harming one another. This was his point in saying that people are not naturally vain and cruel but are made that way by their environment. But this kind of benign indifference to others hardly qualifies as 'nobility' even on the broadest definition. If to be noble means to live up to standards of propriety and self-sacrifice then, obviously, it can exist only in a society that is advanced enough to develop a complicated set of moral precepts and a minimum level of self-awareness. So while Rousseau believed that people in primitive societies are generally happier than those in more advanced ones, they cannot be said to be morally superior. He said, 'since Savage man desires only the things he knows, and knows only the things the possession of which is in his power or easy to achieve, nothing must be so calm as his soul and nothing so limited as his mind' (D 212).

Of course, the question also hinges on what one means by 'savage'. If it refers to the inhabitants of Rousseau's 'pure state of nature' then the idea of a noble savage is absurd, because there is nothing noble about the people and the way of life that he described. If, on the other hand, it refers to people in a more complex state, with language, tools and social structures, but without all of the trappings of modern civilization, then it might make sense to refer to some of them as noble. For example, his discussion of American Indians suggests that he believed some of them to be quite sophisticated morally but without many of the vices of more technologically advanced societies. And he certainly thought that such societies were happier than his own. 'It is most remarkable that for all the years the Europeans have been tormenting themselves to bring the savages of the various parts of the world around to their way of life, they should not yet have been able to win over a single one of them . . . whereas one reads in a thousand places that Frenchmen and other Europeans have voluntarily taken refuge among these nations' (D 219). This outlook can be glimpsed even in his early, unfinished opera from the 1730s, *The Discovery of the New World*.

In any case, the thesis that Rousseau believed in the 'noble savage' comes, I think, from confusion about the meaning of the two 'Discourses'. Because they both trace the gradual corruption of human nature, it is tempting to think that the second 'Discourse' simply extends further back in time the argument from the first 'Discourse'. The first explains how humanity was transformed from ancient Greece to modern France, while the second pushes the theory back to prehistoric times. But this greatly mistakes his meaning in two ways. To begin with, the second 'Discourse' was not straightforwardly historical in the way the first 'Discourse' was, so his depiction of 'natural man' was not simply a theory of what human life was like in the distant past. More importantly, neither work presents a story of mere decline. In the first 'Discourse' he was explicit that his own time was superior to the Middle Ages even if it did not measure up to Sparta and republican Rome (D 6); and in the second he said that 'natural man' was hardly even human at all, because he lacked speech and reason, and certainly it was not a model that one should try to emulate in the present (D 133).

The thesis that unites the two works is that human beings are not inherently and irremediably cruel; rather they have been made that way by their social institutions. The first 'Discourse' explains how the sciences and arts contribute to making human beings morally worse than they need be, while the second 'Discourse' explains, in an abstract way, how the inequalities and suffering of the present world may have come into being, even on the assumption that people are not inherently selfish and vain. Both works criticize modern institutions by comparing them to radical alternatives, either Graeco-Roman antiquity or the state of nature. Yet Rousseau believed that neither of these was an option for his readers. For a time he had some hope that Geneva might cultivate republican virtues and institutions, which is part of the reason he dedicated the second 'Discourse' to his home city. But eventually even this hope was frustrated. Neither the state of nature nor classical antiquity provided a viable formula for improving human life. Rather, they were ideals that helped to diagnose the disease. As for the cure, if it can be called a cure, this was the topic of his two greatest philosophical works, *The Social Contract* and *Emile*.

CHAPTER 4

THE SOCIAL CONTRACT

Rousseau's second 'Discourse' completed his break with the intellectual trends of his age, so after finishing that work in 1754 he made a physical break as well. First he travelled to Geneva, where he reverted to Protestantism and regained his citizenship, and then he and Mlle Levasseur, along with her mother, moved to an isolated cottage outside Paris. Although he received visitors and kept up a large correspondence, the move succeeded in isolating him from the intellectual and social milieu of the capital. The result was a staggering creative outburst. Between the spring of 1756 and the autumn of 1761, he produced a series of masterpieces with a speed and sureness of touch that is perhaps unequalled in literature. These works included his 'Letter to Voltaire on Providence', the novel *Julie*, the 'Letter to D'Alembert on the Theatre' and the two great works that are the topic of this and the next chapter, *The Social Contract* and *Emile*.

BACKGROUND

The full title of the work was *Of the Social Contract, or Principles of Political Right*. Rousseau had begun writing a large work on politics in the 1740s while an assistant to the French ambassador in Venice and had worked on it intermittently over the subsequent two decades. During the key years at the end of the 1750s he returned to it in earnest. 'Of the various works I had on the stocks there was one on which I had long meditated and to which I was more attracted than to the others. To it I was anxious to devote the whole of my life, for it would, in my opinion, put the seal on my reputation. This was my *Political Institutions*. It was thirteen or fourteen years since I had conceived the original idea for it, and at the time I was in Venice and had some opportunity of observing the defects in that Republic's highly vaunted constitution. Since then I had been greatly broadened by my study of the history of morals' (C 377).

Rousseau never completed the full work and *The Social Contract* is the only part of it that he published. In a notice at the beginning he wrote, 'This small treatise is drawn from a larger work, undertaken many years ago without consulting my strength and long since abandoned' (S 40). He was more secretive about this treatise than any of his other published writing, in part because of its highly controversial theories about democracy, political power and religion. In particular, he did not enlist the aid of Diderot, who had been so helpful to him in the writing of the the two 'Discourses'. 'Although I had been engaged in this work for five or six years, I had not got very far with it. Books of this kind require reflection, leisure, and quiet. Besides, I was working on it, as they say, behind closed doors, and I had preferred not to communicate my plan to anyone, even to Diderot. I was afraid that it would seem too bold for the age and the country in which I was writing, and that my friends' alarm might hinder me in the execution' (C 377). When one thinks about the works that were then being published by Diderot, Voltaire, Holbach and others, *The Social Contract* must have seemed outrageous indeed to be judged too bold for its age. It was outrageous, and Rousseau suffered very great persecution as soon as it was published in 1762.

In many ways, this work stands apart from the two 'Discourses' and *Emile*, and in fact Rousseau did not consider it one of his 'principal writings'. Those other works defended the thesis of 'the natural goodness of man' and attempted to show how social institutions corrupt this goodness and make people unhappy and immoral. *The Social Contract* was quite different. It was a contribution to the great debate during the seventeenth and eighteenth centuries about the nature and limits of political obligation, and it took up the classic philosophical topics of sovereignty, citizenship, equality, freedom and justice. Far from defending the 'natural goodness of man', the argument of *The Social Contract* assumes that people are generally selfish and vain, and on this basis it asks what kind of political order can be justified morally.

The obvious differences between this work and his other writings have led some scholars to question whether he even had a coherent philosophy of human nature and politics. Yet although there are apparent contradictions, they are merely superficial. His belief in 'the natural goodness of man' did not imply that most people in present time are virtuous. He often said words to the effect that, 'Men are wicked; a sad and constant experience makes proof unnecessary.' His theory of humanity's natural goodness was compatible with the observation that most people today are immoral, and his other main works were intended precisely to show how this could be so. *The Social Contract* was quite different in that Rousseau began by 'taking men as they are, and laws as they can be' (S 41). This work assumed that people have already been shaped by society and that they possess the character traits that society tends to encourage. From this starting point it went on to investigate the foundation and limits of political power, justice and obligation.

THE ARGUMENT

Rousseau's political philosophy began from the idea expressed in his second 'Discourse' that all political organizations involve coercion. Yet he believed that some forms and uses of public force are more justifiable than others. By the phrase 'principles of political right' in the title of *The Social Contract* he meant the conditions under which coercion would become legitimate and under which citizens would have a moral obligation to obey their rulers. This is an important point because, without it, one is likely to misread the famous opening passages of the book. 'Man is born free, and everywhere he is in chains. One believes himself the others' master, and yet is more a slave than they.' One might infer that in the rest of the book Rousseau would explain how to remove the chains. But this is not the case because political philosophy, on his view, is not a matter of discovering how to remove the chains of coercion, but of discovering what kind of chains, if any, can be morally justified. He continued, 'How did this change come about? I do not know. What can make it legitimate? I believe I can solve this question' (S 41).

The basic thesis of the work was that no person has natural authority over another and that all people are 'created equal' in the sense that no one has political authority just by virtue of his or her name, family or personal merits. While many people take this for granted today it was highly controversial in Rousseau's time, when it was common to believe that God grants to some people authority to tell other people what to do. Since he denied that political authority, and the moral obligation to obey the law, come from nature or God, he thought that it must come from agreements or contracts. In other words, if one person has the right to tell another what to do or not to do, it can only be that the one has granted that power to the other. This was his point in saying that 'the social order is a sacred right, which provides the basis of all the others. Yet this right does not come from nature; it is therefore founded on conventions. The problem is to know what these conventions are' (S 41). As with most of his works, the whole meaning of *The Social Contract* is expressed in its epigraph, 'Let us declare the fair laws of a compact' (S 39).

While his formulation of the point may seem elaborate, the underlying idea is quite familiar. He believed that political authority can only come from 'the consent of the governed'. If one person has the right to command others, and if they in turn have a moral obligation to obey, but if everyone is free and equal to begin with, then that authority can only come about because the people have somehow consented to be ruled in that way. The mechanism by which such consent might be granted is a 'social contract', from which the work takes its name. Such a contract would create a political society by establishing a system of power and obligation based on the consent of the governed. This is why Rousseau is sometimes referred to as a 'contractualist'. A just society must be founded on a social contract, which is to say that it must be founded on consent.

While the ideas of a 'social contract' and the 'consent of the governed' are very familiar today, they raise many philosophical puzzles that Rousseau set out to solve in the first two sections of the work. The most basic of them concerns the terms of a fair social pact. What should the contract stipulate? This is difficult to answer, because consent is a more slippery concept than it first appears. For example, if a person orders another to hand over money at gunpoint, and the second agrees to do so, can one say that the robber has a right to the money because the victim 'consented' to give it to him? There was agreement of a kind, but it was forced, and so presumably the exchange was not genuinely binding. The same logic applies in cases of fraud, where one party is purposely kept in ignorance so they will give their consent to something that they would reject if they knew all the facts. In these cases, one person might agree to something that, afterwards, he is not morally obligated to honour, because the conditions of the agreement were not free and fair.

Thus, Rousseau framed his theory around the question of what political arrangements people would consent to under free and fair conditions. He then argued that it is difficult to specify the terms of such a contract, because the people who enter into it face a dilemma that makes it seem impossible for them to come to an agreement in the first place. To illustrate the point, he imagined what would happen if there were no established government and people decided to form one based on a social contract. He called the condition when there is no government the 'state of nature', but the reader must be careful not to confuse it with the condition described in the early parts of his second 'Discourse', which he called the 'pure state of nature'. The state of nature in *The Social Contract* is the condition that would exist if people were fundamentally as they really are now, but with no government. It is the condition described at the end of the second 'Discourse', which is basically a state of conflict.

In this case, if there were no government, it would be generally irrational to form any contract with other people, because doing so would limits one's options when it came to preserving oneself and one's possessions; thus people who wished to create a social contract faced the following problem: 'This sum of forces can only arise from the cooperation of many: but since each man's force and freedom are his primary instruments of self-preservation, how can he commit them without harming himself?' (S 49). In other words, it is generally irrational to give up one's power and freedom in the state of nature, because these are the best means that one has to ensure one's own well-being, so people cannot easily make the concessions that a social pact requires. He went on to argue, in the most important passage of the work, that in light of this dilemma only one social contract is possible, the stipulations of which are simple, universal and invariable because they 'follow from the nature of things; and are founded on reason' (S 47). Rousseau's way of expressing them was, 'These clauses rightly understood, all come down to just one, namely the total alienation of each associate with all of his rights to the whole community' (S 50).

This means that the only social contract that makes sense is one which requires each party to give up everything to the whole community. The result is that no cases will fall outside the limits of the social contract, and all parties can be certain that their sacrifices will not be taken advantage of by others because there is nothing left by means of which one could injure another. And because each party knows that the other parties submit to the same conditions, the contract is as safe and stable as any can be. The important point is that each party's surrender must be total. 'For if individuals were left some rights, then, since there would be no common superior who might adjudicate between them and the public, each, being judge in his own case on some issue, would soon claim to be so in all' (S 50). By forfeiting all their rights to the community under the direction of the common benefit, the associates reciprocally assure each other that no one can take advantage of another's sacrifice, because no associate retains anything over which the community has no claim. If people retained any such powers, there would be a degree to which they could exploit the sacrifices of others. This would perpetuate the state of nature and the covenant would be meaningless.

The idea that there is only one real, binding social contract is perhaps the most characteristic and important part of Rousseau's political thought. Yet even his defenders might agree that the complete forfeiture of one's power, freedom and possessions to the community seems to be a dreadful arrangement. Moreover, he appeared to enjoy making it seem as onerous as possible: 'Now, the Citizen is no longer judge of the danger the law wills him to risk, and when [the government] has said to him, it is expedient to the state that you die, he ought to die; since it is only on this condition that he has lived in security until then, and his life is no longer only a bounty of nature, but a conditional gift of the state' (S 64). However, his theory of the social pact contained a number of qualifications that make it both more reasonable and less drastic than it appears.

The fundamental issue is why such a total forfeiture is necessary. People today are perhaps more familiar with a competing theory of the social contract, associated with Locke, which states that the citizens of a political society should keep all their rights and prerogatives and only give up to their community the few things necessary for the general good. On this model, the associates agree, for example, to obey the speed limit on the roadways and to pay a fraction of their income for common defence and other public necessities, so that they can keep everything else to themselves to do with as they wish and in a more secure fashion than would be possible on their own.

Yet Rousseau's theory of total alienation had advantages over this theory of partial forfeiture. For all its attractions, the latter faces a problem that cannot be answered on its own terms and to which a theory like Rousseau's offered an adequate solution. To see the problem, one can ask what happens when individual citizens disagree with the political authorities about which powers and possessions the public good requires them to forfeit. Imagine, for example, that a wealthy person does not want to pay taxes to help the less well off, because he believes that the cause of poverty is laziness and that the rich therefore owe nothing to the poor. Then imagine that the government of his community decides that he is wrong and that the social contract requires him to pay more taxes for the benefit of the poor than he thinks he should. The question is, if he wishes to remain a citizen, is he obliged to pay taxes at the level that the law requires, even though he wishes not to and believes it to be unjust?

Presumably the answer is yes, because a political society in which people were not obliged to obey the law would not be a political society at all. But this raises the question of how the state can rightfully demand that the citizen gives something he does not want to give when the authority of the state comes only from the consent of the governed. The only possible answer is that, in some sense, he has already given it. The theory that Rousseau proposed solves this problem by making each associate's forfeiture complete. On this model, when the community taxes its citizens, it is only asking to be returned something that the citizens had already given and which the government had, so to speak, lent back to them. For this reason, Rousseau's theory, which looks odd on the surface, is the more plausible account of the social contract, because it can explain why citizens are obliged to give up certain powers and possessions to the community even when they would prefer not to, something that every political philosophy except anarchism requires, but which the theory of partial forfeiture cannot explain.

The other key difference between Rousseau's theory and that of Locke and other similar philosophers is that Rousseau denied the existence of 'natural rights'. Locke famously argued that even in the state of nature individuals can make moral claims on certain things, such as their own bodies and the fruit of their labour, which other people are morally obliged to respect even if there is no government to enforce it. Locke based his theory on very complicated ideas about the relationship between humanity and God, which Rousseau and most others were unlikely to accept. So Rousseau simplified the theory considerably by arguing that the foundation of all rights is the social pact itself, and that outside it people have few if any moral obligations to each other. This was his point in saying that the social order is the basis of all rights and that it comes not from nature but from conventions, and furthermore that, 'In the state of nature, where everything is common, I owe nothing to those to whom I have promised nothing. I recognize as another's only what is of no use to myself' (S 66).

Rousseau famously went on to argue that while everyone forfeits everything under the social pact, each gets everything back in a higher form, 'they acquire everything they have given' (S 56). While this may appear to be a sophism, the point is sound. Private property offers a simple example, for if property is a possession to which an owner has a unique right, then strictly speaking there is no property in the state of nature. In the social pact, however, since everyone forfeits everything, there is nothing left by means of which anyone can claim special privilege, so possessions from the state of nature revert back to their possessors in the form of property to which they are entitled by the terms of the covenant, and which the combined forces of the community are obliged to protect. A party to the contract loses 'the unlimited right to everything that tempts him and he can reach', but gains 'property in everything he possesses' (S 54). Furthermore, 'What is remarkable about this alienation is that the community, far from despoiling individuals of their goods by accepting them, only secures to them their legitimate possession, changes usurpation into genuine rights, and use into property' (S 56).

Everything in *The Social Contract* flows from his account of the social pact and the remainder of the book thus has a remarkable coherence and tightness in its argument. To begin, there is his theory of sovereignty and the concept of the 'general will'. Rousseau argued that since the associates to the social contract agree to subordinate themselves to the good of the community, some instrument is necessary to determine what that good consists of. This is the role that he assigned to the Sovereign, which is his somewhat misleading term for the law-making body within political society. The purpose of the law is to declare what kinds of actions will be required or forbidden in order to promote the well-being of the community, to which the citizens have pledged themselves (S 61). The job of the Sovereign is, 'the specification, by various particular laws, of the actions that contribute to this greatest good [of all]' (S 160). To express the idea of the greatest good of all he often used the term 'general will', which stands in opposition to the 'particular will' or the good of some person or group within the community (S 52–3, 57).

He then went on to argue that the Sovereign can be no one but the people themselves, or the members of the social pact, which is to say that the political society must be governed democratically. This was obviously a controversial argument in his time, especially in France, with its tradition of grand monarchy. Two distinctions are needed to understand this point, one of which makes it seem even more radical, but the other less so. First, when Rousseau argued that the people must vote on their own laws, he meant that the people themselves must vote, not just their representatives. His theory of democracy was an argument for direct rather than representative democracy. This was his point in saying that, 'Sovereignty cannot be represented . . . Any law which the People has not ratified in person is null; it is not a law' (S 114), and that, 'the instant a People gives itself Representatives, it ceases to be free; it ceases to be' (S 115). It was also the basis of his criticism of the English parliamentary system. 'The English people thinks it is free; it is greatly mistaken, it is free only during the election of Members of Parliament; as soon as they are elected it is enslaved, it is nothing. The use it makes of its freedom during the brief moments it has it fully warrants its losing it' (S 114).

The second point is that when Rousseau argued that sovereignty cannot be represented, he meant something very specific by the word sovereignty. His constitutional theory identified a number of different offices in a well-ordered society, the two most important being the Sovereign and (as he called it) the Prince, which correspond roughly to the legislative and executive parts of the state. His argument against representation applied only to the first; the people cannot give up their sovereign power of making the law. Regarding the executive branch, however, he said that the people not only can but also should elect representatives (S 93). This means that his argument for direct democracy was not a call to return to the ancient democracies of Greece and Rome, in which the people were permanently assembled not only to frame the law but also to declare war, negotiate treaties, try court cases, watch over the public accounts and perform all the other functions of government.

The other crucial concept in his theory of political authority is the 'general will', which is somewhat hard to pin down. The basic idea is that a group or society has a will of its own that is independent of the desires of particular citizens. For example, say that an enemy army is massing at the borders in preparation for an invasion. The good of the community, as an association of citizens persisting through time, includes as its first principle the self-preservation of the community which at this moment requires that able-bodied persons go to the border to defend the homeland. This is the 'general will' or the will of the community as such. Yet it is not necessarily what each person wants, or even what any person wants, because it may not be to the individual person's benefit to go to the border. It is much safer to stay away from the fighting, plus if the nation is overrun the draft-dodger might be able to plead a better case to the invading power.

In this example, the person's particular will, which is to shirk his duty, may be at odds with the general will, which requires that he defend his country. However, the particular will need not always deviate from the general will, even when the person involved is very selfish. If the particular will and general will did not overlap on at least some occasions, then political society would never have come into being in the first place, 'for while the opposition of particular interests made the establishment of society necessary, it is the agreement of these same interests which made it possible' (S 57). Furthermore, people can be taught to define their own good in terms of fulfilling their obligations to others, which makes the contract stronger, and which Rousseau believed should be the goal of public education (S 69).

While it may seem odd to say that a group of people can have a will that is different from the will of some or even all of its members, the same principle is evident in many kinds of collective action. A sports team, for example, may have the general will of winning games, yet a particular player might do best for herself by sitting out even at the price of a victory. Perhaps at a crucial point in a game the team could use her service, yet she might have an injury that will be aggravated by her participation, causing her suffering later in life. Business corporations offer many similar examples. The business might be organized with the general will of making profits, while a particular employee's good might be served by spending time with his family rather than working long hours to make the business more lucrative for someone else.

In both cases, the group is nothing but the individuals who make it up, yet it can have a conventional, collective will that is different from their wills taken as individuals. This was Rousseau's point in distinguishing between the 'general will' and the 'will of all' (S 60). Yet many questions remain, because it is unclear whether the term refers to something purely abstract, analogous to 'the good life' or 'well-being', or to something concrete about the good of a particular community in a particular time and place. Similarly, it is unclear whether an ideal observer could at least in principle discover the general will independently of the judgement of the political community in question; or whether the general will is nothing other than the properly qualified and aggregated judgement of that community.

In addition to sovereignty, law and the general will, a third important idea is that of the Prince, which is another one of Rousseau's slightly misleading terms. The Prince, again, is Rousseau's name for the executive branch of the political authority, which enacts the laws passed by the legislature (S 82–6). These two offices, the Sovereign and the Prince, are the most important parts of the institutional structure that he described. He argued that they are necessary elements of any well-ordered society and that they define the character of the political life within the social pact. The nature of each is easy enough to understand; yet their relationship to each other raises interesting paradoxes in his theory of government. For he argued that the Sovereign, namely the people themselves, should be the supreme power in the state and carefully check the executive branch, yet the mechanism for doing so is left somewhat hazy (S 118–20).

A further element in his theory of the state is the Lawgiver, which is one of the most interesting and difficult parts of his political philosophy (S 68). Rousseau argued that the social pact requires that the people who enter into it have a certain kind of character if the pact is to succeed. They must have at least some minimal feelings of patriotism, cooperativeness and public spirit. Yet, they cannot get these qualities from the political society itself, because they are necessary conditions for such a society to come into being in the first place. Thus there must be something outside, and prior to, the social pact that forms its members into potential citizens; Rousseau's name for this entity is the Lawgiver. The most important thing to realize is that, on his theory, the Lawgiver does not actually make the law, a fact that can be confusing. In his technical usage, the term law refers only to the decisions of the Sovereign regarding the actions that will be compelled or forbidden in the name of the general will. Conversely, the

Lawgiver establishes the conditions of political society, but has no authority to pass laws within that society. 'This office which gives the republic its constitution has no place in its constitution' (S 69).

A final interesting and difficult aspect of his political philosophy is the theory of 'moral freedom'. While it has been the topic of much debate and confusion, the root idea is fairly clear and very powerful. In the civil society he described, the nature of human actions changes from what it was in the state of nature, because people are obliged to ask themselves not, 'What do I want to do?' but, 'What am I supposed to do based on the terms of the social pact that I have entered?' The possibility of asking this question, a possibility that did not exist in the state of nature, shows that a change has taken place in the kind of beings that humans are. His full statement on the issue was, 'This transition from the state of nature to the civil state produces a most remarkable change in man by substituting justice for instinct in his conduct, and endowing his actions with the morality they previously lacked. Only then, when the voice of duty succeeds physical compulsion and right succeeds appetite, does man, who until then had looked only to himself, see himself forced to act on other principles, and to consult his reason before listening to his inclinations' (S 53). 'Moral freedom' was his term for this power of acting according to duty.

The background of his thesis is a familiar argument in the history of philosophy. It says that a person's passions or appetites derive ultimately from the condition of that person's body; and, further, the body is a part of the physical world that is governed by the same natural necessities that govern all physical processes. Thus, when one acts only according to one's passions, one is a kind of undifferentiated part of the material world, governed by the same natural laws that apply to all other physical systems. In Rousseau's words, 'I see in every animal nothing but an ingenious machine to which nature has given sense in order to wind itself up and, to a point, protect itself against everything that tends to destroy or to disturb it' (D 140). He assumed, further, that actions that happen according to mere natural necessity have no moral significance. For example, if a child falls and gets hurt, no one blames the force of gravity, although they might blame the parents if they believe the parents were able to prevent it. The implication is that the state of nature is inherently amoral, because everything that happens is the product of natural necessity alone.

When people enter the social pact, however, the nature of their actions changes. The social pact itself is an instance of self-legislation, which provides a new basis for action; it gives people a rule to follow apart from their particular inclinations. Furthermore, once it is enacted the community will begin to frame laws, which further stipulate the citizens' obligations to one another, and which serve as further rules for action. The social pact thus enables people to act on the basis of their political duties rather than on the basis of drives that nature has, so to speak, forced upon them. Rousseau argued that this possibility raises each citizen out of the mere play of natural forces and endows their actions with a kind of moral significance that they would otherwise lack, although he said little about how this transformation might actually take place. Similarly, this was his point in saying that, 'whoever refuses to obey the general will shall be constrained to do so by the entire body: which means nothing other than he shall be forced to be free' (S 53). While readers never tire of interpreting this comment in sinister ways, Rousseau's point was a simple one. Any citizen who breaks the community's law also breaks the social pact and thus, by the nature of the case, violates the law that he has legislated for himself. To punish him is simply to force him to obey rules he freely set for himself.

This line of thought has important consequences for Rousseau's theory of moral freedom. One is that being free, in the sense of being autonomous, has nothing to do with feeling free. Once the social pact is enacted, self-legislation applies more to the form of action than to the feelings of the agent. The criterion for freedom is whether or not an action is in conformity with the law that one has erected over oneself. If it is, then the act is autonomous on Rousseau's definition. Thus, for example, if the common good demands that an individual gives up some of his or her property to the use of the community, the freedom that is implied in this forfeiture has nothing to do with whether or not the person in question wants to do it. Autonomy is defined by conformity to the law that the person has enacted as a form of self-legislation.

In the first two Books of *The Social Contract*, Rousseau defined the basic political structure that would follow from the terms of his social pact. In the second two he went on to discuss details of government and policy within this constitutional framework. No part of his discussion is more interesting, or was more controversial, than his discussion of religion and politics in Book IV. He combined an extraordinary respect for individual conscience with an equal commitment to the common good. 'Subjects therefore only owe the Sovereign an account of their opinions in so far as those opinions matter to the community. Now it certainly matters to the State that each Citizen have a religion which makes him love his duties; but the dogmas of this Religion are only of concern to the State or its members in so far as the dogmas bear on morality' (S 150). In other words, people should be free to believe anything they want as long as what they believe does not harm the community.

The interesting thing about Rousseau's theory is that he put equal emphasis on both stipulations. He argued that because people are generally selfish, there must be some kind of broad civil profession of faith with tenets stating that a providential God exists and that in the next life the good will be rewarded and the wicked punished; and furthermore, he said that, 'the Sovereign may banish from the state anyone who does not believe them' (S 150). Yet he also argued that, 'Beyond this everyone may hold whatever opinion he pleases, without its being up to the Sovereign to know them . . . whatever the subjects' fate may be in the time to come is none of its business, provided they are good citizens in this life' (S 150). He went on to say, 'Now that there no longer is and no longer can be an exclusive national Religion, one must tolerate all those which tolerate others in so far as their dogmas contain nothing contrary to the duties of the Citizen' (S 151). While Rousseau seemed to be walking a fine line in these passages, his account of civil religion follows directly from the principles articulated in Books I and II.

His defence of a mandatory profession of faith suggests to many scholars today that Rousseau was not serious about civil liberty and religious toleration. While this is something that readers must decide for themselves, one should at least understand his meaning and motivation. He argued that since the preservation of society is the condition for having any rights at all, one cannot meaningfully have a right to something that tends towards the destruction of society. Because certain beliefs are destructive in this way, the state may do what it can to prevent them or at least to prevent their spread. This may or may not seem acceptable, yet two considerations are worth bearing in mind. The first is that every defence of individual liberty eventually bumps into the question of how to deal with beliefs and behaviours that are destructive of the system of liberties itself. Even Locke, who is usually considered to be a more ardent defender of individual liberty than Rousseau, argued that religious toleration could not be extended to Catholics and atheists, because their beliefs are destructive of the political system that guarantees individual liberty in the first place. Rousseau said nothing more than this.

Furthermore, Rousseau might simply have been wrong about what beliefs are necessary for the preservation of society, in which case his principles would offer no grounds for the kind of persecution in question. In the case of atheism, his argument was quite clear. He believed that the weakness of the human will is such that people who do not fear punishment and hope for reward in the afterlife are unlikely to perform their civic responsibilities in this one; thus atheism is destructive of political society and should not be tolerated. His argument against extending toleration to Catholics followed these same lines, but was a little more complicated because it fell into two parts. The first was that since Catholics believe that the pope is literally Christ's vicar on earth, they can never be citizens of any state except the one ruled by the pope himself, because sovereignty cannot be divided. He said that Roman Catholicism is a religion which, 'by giving men two legislators, two chiefs, two fatherlands, subjects them to contradictory duties and prevents their being at once devout and Citizens' (S 146–47). His second argument against the toleration of Catholicism was that since the state must protect civil liberties it cannot tolerate religions that are themselves intolerant of other creeds. In particular, people who believe that their Church is the only means to salvation are dangerous to society because 'it is impossible to live in peace with people one believes to be damned'. For this reason, 'whoever dares to say, *no Salvation outside the Church*, has to be driven out of the State; unless the State is the Church, and the Prince the Pontiff. Such a dogma is good only in Theocratic Government, in any other it is pernicious' (S 151).

The important thing to realize, again, is that Rousseau may have been wrong about what beliefs are necessary to preserve society. In the case of atheism, the question of whether a society of atheists is possible was one of the classic questions of Enlightenment political philosophy and it is not clear that Rousseau's side had the better arguments. The question of Catholicism is more difficult, because there has often been controversy over the authority of the pope and the possibility of salvation outside the Church. Yet at least one point is obvious. Rousseau certainly went too far in saying that one cannot live in peace with those whom one believes to be damned. His reasoning was that, 'to love them would be to hate God who punishes them; one must absolutely bring them back [to the fold] or torment them' (S 151).

This ignores two points; there is a traditional view that one can hate the sin but love the sinner, and in any case there are other ways to save souls in the next life besides tormenting them in this one. This latter point raises the tricky question of how the right to proselytize fits in with the right to other kinds of expression; yet the basic insight remains. Rousseau may have been wrong about what beliefs preserve society; and if he was wrong about atheists and Catholics then nothing in his philosophy would justify their persecution; indeed their views would be protected under the same principles that protect all other kinds of individual freedom. One must bear these considerations in mind in making a correct evaluation of his theory of religious toleration.

THE RESPONSE

While Rousseau's political philosophy was undoubtedly radical in its doctrine of total alienation, its defence of democracy and its criticisms of Catholicism, it still fitted within a recognizable tradition of social contract theories that could trace their lineage back through Hobbes or even Plato. By the middle of the eighteenth century, however, that tradition had come under devastating attack by philosophers like David Hume. To some degree, Rousseau had learned from the past and his theory of the social pact avoided many of the philosophical difficulties that had trapped his predecessors. Yet Hume's objections were so broad in scope that they posed problems for all contractualist theories, even one as sophisticated as Rousseau's. Most of these objections were set forth in Hume's 1748 essay 'Of the Original Contract', and have been the topic of debate throughout the intervening centuries. Although I doubt that Rousseau could answer all of them adequately, they help to clarify the intentions and limits of his theory.

Perhaps the most obvious problem with his theory is that it derives all political rights and obligations from a social contract, yet there never was such a contract in the history of the world. Indeed, most political philosophies that make use of the idea of a social pact face the problem that it never happened. Furthermore, even in the rare case of a nation like the United States that did begin in a social pact, only a tiny minority of those whom it claimed to govern actually gave their assent to it. After all, only a small percentage of the population was allowed to vote on the Constitution in the first place, namely the members of the various ratifying conventions; and many of them voted against it. Furthermore, those delegates were themselves elected by the small minority of the total population consisting mostly of white, male landholders.

Therefore it is unclear why the people who voted against it or were not allowed to vote at all, together making up almost the entire population, should have been required to obey principles whose moral force, according to Rousseau, comes only from their being assented to. And even if there were an answer to the question, it would not explain why future generations exist under the writ of the contract given that they were not even born when it was made. And all this without mentioning the obvious fact that the terms of the Constitution of the United States, along with every other existing constitution, are nothing like the social contract that Rousseau advocated, even though he argued that the 'clauses of this contract are so completely determined by the nature of the act that the slightest modification would render them null and void' (S 50).

All theories of politics based on a social contract face this knot of difficulties, and it has special force for Rousseau's theory, which defined the terms of the social pact so narrowly. The usual way to answer this is by a theory of tacit consent, according to which people can be said to consent to things that they never explicitly agreed to or even understood. But this kind of argument is notoriously tricky. For example, people often say that if a person stays in his country and accepts the benefit of the laws, then he has tacitly consented to be a member of that political society even if he was given no vote on its founding principles; thus, the government still rules by the consent of the governed even though the governed never consented to anything. However, this line of argument whittles the idea of consent down to nothing. As Hume asked, 'Can we seriously say, that a poor peasant or artizan has a free choice to leave his country, when he knows no foreign language or manners, and lives from day to day, by the small wages he acquires?' If so, he continued, then, 'We may as well assert, that a man, by remaining in a vessel, freely consents to the dominion of the master; though he was carried on board while asleep, and must leap into the ocean, and perish, the moment he leaves her.'

While this is a powerful objection to some theories of the social contract, it has little effect for Rousseau's, because he was clear that the contract he described was not intended to depict a historical or factual event. The social pact functioned as an ideal about the terms under which abstract rational agents could put bonds of obligation upon themselves. It functioned, in other words, as an abstraction in light of which one may better understand the nature and justification of existing institutions, although none of them began in a contract of the kind he described. One may question, however, how such an ideal theory of the social pact can help to understand the nature and justification of real political institutions.

Rousseau did not imagine that at some time long ago people came together and arranged their political affairs along the lines described in *The Social Contract*. Rather, the contract shows the terms under which a political union might be voluntarily entered into instead of being imposed against the wishes and interests of its subjects. In this sense the social contract is an ideal for society in light of which one can judge existing institutions. His reader can compare its terms to the ones that seem to be embodied in actual political arrangements and thereby learn something about the nature and justification of those arrangements. In this sense the social pact had an ideal function similar to that of the theory of the 'pure state of nature' in the second 'Discourse'. Rousseau himself described its purpose by analogy to the physicist's is use of ideal motion across ideal surfaces. In explaining the path of a body in motion, a physicist might begin with the idea of movement across a frictionless surface. Now, as a matter of fact, there may be no frictionless surfaces anywhere in the universe, and even the idea of one may be contradictory. But the ideal of such a surface, even though it does not exist and perhaps could not exist, provides a kind of principle in light of which one may better understand what actually happens. Similarly, the social contract functions as an ideal in light of which one may understand the real.

Hume's other objections, however, are more difficult to resolve in the terms of Rousseau's theory. The second objection concerns the conditions under which the social contract is made. Rousseau argued that all political obligation comes from the consent of the governed, but this does not imply that people are obliged to do everything that they consent to do. The conditions under which people give their consent are also relevant because, again, people are presumably not bound to their agreements in cases involving force and fraud. Rousseau granted this point, as for example in his depiction of the origin of law in the second 'Discourse', where he said that it is a trick played by the rich on the poor, which is no more legitimate because the poor foolishly agreed to it (D 173). This is also the basis of his argument against Aristotle on the question of whether some people are slaves by nature. Rousseau claimed that even if some people do agree to remain slaves even when freedom is offered, their consent is not genuine because their prior, involuntary servitude has robbed them of their power to make free and informed choices. Thus, Rousseau should have stated the conditions that must exist for the social pact to be legitimate.

But he did not do so clearly. The simple answer is to say that consent brings obligation when it is offered under conditions that are free and fair, which is to say conditions that are not coerced. The social pact is binding, on this reading, because the associates agree to it under conditions that are themselves fair; yet if this is the answer that he intended to give, then his theory seems to be in trouble. The most important part of his account of the state of nature in *The Social Contract* was that people have no natural duties to each other, which is why all obligations are based on consent. But if there are no principles of obligation outside the social pact, then it is not clear how one can specify the fair conditions under which the pact should be made in order to bring such obligations into existence. Without a theory of natural rights and duties, it seems that everything is equally fair in the state of nature, because everyone has 'an unlimited right to everything that tempts him'. If the social pact determines what is fair then it is impossible to say that it must be created under conditions that are themselves fair.

In some passages he seemed to offer a solution to this objection; but it led to the opposite problem. His answer was to say that the social pact does not actually create principles of justice, it only confers the authority to enforce them. Indeed, this is what he seemed to mean by saying, 'What is good and conformable to order is so by the nature of things and independently of human conventions. All justice comes from God, he alone is its source . . . [but considering] things in human terms, the laws of justice are vain among men for want of natural sanctions' (S 66). This reading has the advantage of explaining what it means to say that the social contract must be made under free and fair terms, because those terms would be the ones consistent with the natural principles of justice. But this raises the opposite problem from above.

If there are natural principles of justice, then what could it mean to say that in the state of nature 'I owe nothing to those to whom I have promised nothing'? Presumably one would owe to others whatever the natural principles of justice require; otherwise they would not be principles of justice in the first place. In short, either principles of justice exist outside the social pact or they do not. If they do not, then it is not clear that Rousseau can distinguish the sort of consent that produces real obligations from that which does not. If they do, then it is not clear he can argue that there are no natural duties and that all obligations are founded on the social pact. He certainly leaned towards the side which says that the social pact creates justice instead of merely enforcing it, as is required by his argument that a person owes nothing to those whom he has promised nothing. Yet, it seems he also sensed the difficulties raised by such a radically voluntaristic theory.

A third objection is related to the previous one and is no less powerful for being obvious. If all obligations are founded on covenants or promises, why then are the associates obliged to keep their promises in the first place? For example, in a political society of the kind Rousseau described, the associates would be required to respect each other's property. If someone raises the question of why she is obliged to do so, the answer would be that such respect is due by the terms of the social contract to which she had given her consent and promise to obey. But if she further asks why she should keep her promises, there is a problem. If all obligations are based on promises then there is nothing outside the pact in reference to which it is obligatory to keep one's promise to obey the terms of the pact itself. Or, if there is some such thing, then promises are unnecessary as foundations for political obligations, and so the whole social contract is redundant. As Hume argued, 'Besides this, I say, you find yourself embarrassed, when it is asked, *why we are bound to keep our word*? Nor can you give any answer, but what would, immediately, without any circuit, have accounted for our obligation to allegiance.'

There is a final objection to Rousseau's theory of the social pact, one that Hume did not discuss, but which is exceptionally important in light of much contemporary political philosophy. The social contract is as an idealized agreement between abstract rational agents in a hypothetical circumstance called the state of nature. Its purpose is to reveal the principles that reasonable agents might use to create a political society by uniting themselves through ties of mutual obligations. It is an abstract ideal in light of which one might better understand the nature and justification of existing political institutions; and Rousseau's general line of argument may be understood by comparing his use of the state of nature and the social contract to a physicist's use of ideas such as a frictionless surface. Yet these last two cases are not exactly analogous; and this is the source of a problem.

The physicist's theory, like Rousseau's theory in the second 'Discourse', is purely descriptive and explanatory; specifically, it is designed to describe and predict the paths of bodies in motion, such as billiard balls on a table. This means that the ultimate test of an abstract notion such as a frictionless surface is whether it allows one to predict the phenomena in question in an accurate and wide-ranging way. Rousseau's theory of the social pact was not quite like this, however, because it is normative rather than descriptive. He intended to explain not what is the case, but what ought to be the case. In this light it is not clear what can count as evidence for or against his theory, because it is a theory of what is not so, but should be so. In other words, one can certainly ask whether the social contract he described is a rational and reasonable thing for hypothetical people in a hypothetical state of nature to engage in; but since those circumstances are hypothetical, their relevance to existing people and institutions is unclear in as much as they are intended to yield normative conclusions about what real citizens owe to real governments, and vice versa.

Perhaps these problems cannot be answered in the terms that Rousseau's philosophy offered. In any case, to the extent that this reading is correct, many of the problems have the same source in his philosophy, namely his effort to combine two doctrines that do not go easily together. He wished to argue both that people have no natural duties to one another and that once political society is established they have obligations that go beyond mere prudence, or calculations of enlightened self-interest. Each of these is enormously attractive taken by itself, which makes Rousseau's effort to combine them something of enduring philosophical interest. In fact, it may be that the only way to do so is by means of a theory like Rousseau's that bases obligation on covenants. Even if he failed to solve the problem completely, his efforts clarified the nature of the case, and showed the questions that any theory will face in trying to base political authority on a social contract.

Another facet of Rousseau's theory that has received searching and profound criticism is his theory of direct democracy. The doctrine is certainly strange. The most obvious problem is that it implies that no state can have a larger number of citizens than can practicably meet to discuss the law. He said that he planned to discuss this problem in the sequel to *The Social Contract*, but he never completed that work. It seems that his plan would have involved confederations of very small states (S 111, 116). Whatever his solution, however, this issue makes it hard to know what he would have said about the modern nation state with its millions or billions of citizens. It appears that if he was serious in saying that the terms of the social pact are invariable (S 50), that they are the only source of obligation (S 44) and that they require direct democracy (S 114), then no modern nation state can claim allegiance from its citizens. At one point he seemed to say as much himself. 'Since the law is nothing but the declaration of the general will, it is clear that the people cannot be represented in its legislative power . . . This shows that, upon closer examination, very few Nations would be found to have laws' (S 115). While this is somewhat discouraging, one should note that if he happened to be correct about the nature and foundations of political obligation, and therefore correct about direct democracy, he cannot be held responsible if people have decided to organize themselves around other principles.

Benjamin Constant raised a more substantial set of objections to Rousseau's theory of democracy in a famous speech of 1816 called 'The Liberty of the Ancients Compared with that of the Moderns'. His thesis was that although the citizens of modern republics are as intense in their love of freedom as were the ancient Greeks and Romans, these two groups, the moderns and the ancients, in fact loved two different things. Today people think of freedom in terms of individual rights, whereas in ancient times they thought of it as collective self-rule. Regarding modern freedom, he said that it is the right 'of everyone to express their opinion, choose a profession and practise it, to dispose of property, and even to abuse it; to come and go without permission, and without having to account for their motives or undertakings. It is everyone's right to associate with other individuals'. Among the Greeks and Romans, on the other hand, liberty meant democracy; it 'consisted in exercising collectively, but

· directly, several parts of the complete sovereignty; in deliberating, in the public square, over war and peace; in forming alliances with other governments; in voting laws, in pronouncing judgments'. Constant went on to argue that these two kinds of freedom (individual liberty and democracy) are incompatible. While his reasoning was complicated, two of his arguments are especially relevant. The first reason that democracy is incompatible with civil liberty is that the only way to leave citizens the leisure to attend continually to public affairs is to have a slave population to do the work, something that is obviously inconsistent with modern liberty to the degree that it is described in terms of universal rights. Constant defined ancient liberty not simply as a general concern with public affairs but as actual self-rule, which can only be accomplished when the whole body of citizens has the time to administer the state's business. Thus, 'the abolition of slavery has deprived the free population of all the leisure which resulted from the fact that slaves took care of most of the work. Without the slave population of Athens, 20,000 Athenians could never have spent every day at the public square in discussion.' Rousseau, by the way, made the same argument saying, 'What! Freedom can only be maintained with the help of servitude? Perhaps. The two extremes meet. Everything that is not in nature has its inconveniences, and civil society more than all the rest' (S 115).

Constant also suggested another reason that a democratic state cannot offer broad individual liberties, although his argument was less explicit in this case. He said that democracy requires a very specific kind of citizenry in order to function, and thus it cannot offer too much individual freedom. The people must be public-spirited, informed, patriotic, skilled in analysis and debate and willing to sacrifice themselves for the public good. He said, 'The ancients . . . had no notion of individual rights. Men were, so to speak, merely machines, whose gears and cog-wheels were regulated by the law. The same subjection characterized the golden centuries of the Roman republic; the individual was in some ways lost in the nation, the citizen in the city.' Yet this requirement is obviously incompatible with broad individual liberty, because people who must possess such a specific kind of character cannot, by the nature of the case, be free to believe, feel and desire whatever they want. This same issue appeared in Rousseau in his discussion of the Lawgiver.

There is of course a further difficulty in the relationship between civil liberty and democracy, which Constant did not say much about but which is important to understanding Rousseau. Democracies often put strict limits on the civil freedoms of the people they claim to rule. Sometimes these are uniformly imposed (such as in Rousseau's Geneva where even the ruling classes had very little in the way of civil liberties), whereas at other times these limits apply only to a subgroup of the population, such as laws that discriminate against women or minorities. The point is the same in both cases, however. Democratic governments often democratically choose not to allow broad individual liberties. Thus, people who wish to defend both individual liberty and democracy must put them in rank order and decide which should be sacrificed to the other. This is a serious problem, which has caused some philosophers to ask whether liberal democracy is a self-contradictory theory of government. And it is not even to ask the more fundamental question of what partisans of democracy would have to say about a state that democratically chooses to be no longer governed democratically.

In sum, Constant argued that because democracy requires slavery and because it demands that the people be moulded into citizen-machines, it cannot coexist with broad individual freedom. What is very illuminating in this is the severe fault that Constant found with Rousseau for, to put it simply, he accused Rousseau of trying to rekindle ancient liberty in the modern world, with disastrous results. Constant believed that people today must be content with individual liberty and not try too much to reconstitute the democracy of ancient times. Changes in communication, trade and warfare, along with the progress of the idea that all people are worthy of equal respect, have made it impossible to return to small, independent republics that rely on slavery. He said, 'we can no longer enjoy the liberty of the ancients, which consisted in active and constant participation in the collective power. Our freedom must consist of peaceful enjoyment and private independence.' Furthermore, he argued that the attempt to reinstitute direct democracy could come only at the terrible price of undoing the modern nation state, commerce and individual liberty.

He claimed that Rousseau's theory regarding the need for people to vote personally for their own laws was an attempt to resurrect ancient liberty in the modern world. 'I shall show that, by transposing into our modern age an extent of social power, of collective sovereignty, which belonged to other centuries, this sublime genius, animated by the purest love of liberty, has nevertheless furnished

deadly pretexts for more than one kind of tyranny.' Having partici-
pated in many tumultuous years of French political life at the turn
of the nineteenth century, Constant was in a better position than
most to gauge the influence of Rousseau's theories. Yet, in terms of
what Rousseau himself intended, he was incorrect. For Rousseau's
defence of democracy against excessive individual liberty was
extremely nuanced and qualified.

To begin with, Rousseau was himself concerned with preserving a
domain of civil liberty within which people could pursue their own
interests, as was clear in his discussion of religious toleration. Yet
Constant was right in sensing that he and Rousseau balanced things
differently; and this difference puts the meaning of Rousseau's
theory of democracy in a clear light. For if individual liberty and
democracy are both good things, and if they are inherently in
tension with one another as both thinkers believed, then any political philosophy ought to provide an account of which should be
sacrificed to the other and when. The easiest way to understand the
difference between Constant and Rousseau is that the former was
more willing than the latter to sacrifice democracy for the sake of
individual liberty. Yet Rousseau did not go to the other extreme; he
did not simply sacrifice individual rights to democracy. In fact, just
as his theory of civil liberty attempted to reconcile a robust defence
of individual rights with a plausible theory of sovereignty, so his
account of democracy tried to reconcile that same theory of rights
with the need for collective self-government.

While readers must decide for themselves whether one should err
on the side of individual liberties or democracy, a few last points will
clarify Rousseau's position. The first is that his defence of democracy was highly qualified. The most obvious limit was that he recommended democracy only for the framing of legislation; he argued
that all other government functions should be delegated to representatives, which means that his theory does not require the people
to be perpetually assembled to attend to public affairs. Furthermore
he defended a view of civil liberty that was much more expansive
than anything found in ancient political philosophy. This shows that
Constant was wrong in suggesting that Rousseau wished to return
the modern world to the Greek city-states. Moreover, Constant and
many modern readers criticize Rousseau's theory of democracy as if
it were something he chose because he liked it, as if it were a matter
of taste. It is hard to know what to make of this kind of objection,

however, because Rousseau himself, at least, believed that the argument for direct democracy was a necessary consequence of the terms of the social pact, which were themselves necessary. So it makes little sense to blame him for his conclusion. He may have been wrong, of course; but even if he was, it was not exactly a moral failing given that he seems to have tried his best and done better than most to discover the foundation of political authority.

Finally, Constant and Rousseau agreed on one further issue, which has consequences for how one evaluates Rousseau's theory of democracy and individual rights. Both thinkers argued that the greatest threat to a well-ordered society is the indifference of its citizens. Human nature is such that people with power tend to use it to their own advantage; so that if the people are not vigilant towards their leaders the government will become self-serving. Although Constant argued that people in the modern world must be satisfied with individual rights instead of political participation, he defended representative democracy, as opposed to monarchy, because it gives the people some measure of oversight of their rulers. Yet this raises the question of whether the citizens' increasing obsession with the enjoyment of their private rights, which he applauded, will render them less willing and able to attend to public affairs. Even Constant worried about this. 'The danger of modern liberty is that, absorbed in the enjoyment of our private independence, and in the pursuit of our particular interests, we should surrender our right to share in political power too easily. The holders of authority are only too anxious to encourage us to do so.' In this regard, Rousseau and Constant were both especially concerned about the role of commerce, which they thought tended to detach people further from the public good. The question remains whether Constant's representative system based on individual rights requires sufficient participation to keep its citizens sufficiently knowledgeable and attentive to restrain the corruption of politicians.

Yet none of these objections, neither Hume's searching criticism of Rousseau's theory of the social contract nor Constant's arguments against his theory of direct democracy, touches the most famous and devastating charge that is lodged against Rousseau. Many able scholars have argued that *The Social Contract* cleared the way for totalitarianism. The sources of this charge are easy to find. As mentioned before, Rousseau did say that, 'when [the government] has said to him, it is expedient to the state that you die, he ought to die; since it is only on this condition that he has lived in security until then, and his life is no longer only a bounty of nature, but a conditional gift of the state' and that citizens will be 'forced to be free' (S 64, 53). And referring to the role of the Lawgiver he said, 'Anyone who dares to institute a people must feel capable of, so to speak, changing human nature; of transforming each individual who by himself is a perfectly solitary whole into part of a larger whole from which the individual would as it were receive his life and his being' (S 69). These passages suggest that he believed that individuals should be completely submerged into the state with no room left for individual liberty.

This line of criticism has been advanced by some of Rousseau's most capable readers including Jacob Talmon, Isaiah Berlin and Daniel Bell, the last of whom put it this way. 'The problem, as Rousseau put it, was that in modern society man was both *bourgeois* and *citoyen*. As a citizen he had public duties, but as a bourgeois he pursued private interests, appetites, and passions. Rousseau sought to overcome this bifurcation in *The Social Contract* . . . by the denial of all private individual interests, the erasure of all ego into the single moral personality which would be the community or the general will. Without self-interest, each person would be equal to every other in all respects. In contemporary life, this alternative is exemplified in Communist China, and its civil religion – which Rousseau also thought necessary as a binding belief – in the deification of Mao's thought.' Yet despite the extraordinary intelligence of these scholars, their criticism is misguided.

As mentioned above, *The Social Contract* described a hypothetical agreement between abstract rational agents who wished to make their lives more secure by placing bonds of mutual obligation upon themselves whereby each would help the other in times of need. The book described the terms and implications of such a social contract, and went on to explain its consequences for such issues as sovereignty, justice and religion. The essence of the social pact is that it treats all members as free and equal, because any party who was disadvantaged by it would not consent to enter in the first place. Now, it is true that the political community would then make claims on the power, time, possessions and perhaps lives of its members, but that is, after all, the point of creating a political society: the members help each other. But he also argued that in all those matters that are not relevant to the community, the state must be silent and individuals left alone.

Because the pact requires citizens to give up the power to do those things that are inconsistent with the common good, they lose their 'natural freedom' but gain 'civil freedom' or the freedom that comes from being protected against harm both from outsiders and from one's fellow citizens. Rousseau wrote, '*In the Republic*, says M. d'A[rgenson] *everyone is perfectly free with respect to what does not harm others.* That is the invariable boundary, it cannot be drawn more accurately' (S 150, note). Of course this leaves it up to the community, the citizens themselves, to decide what does and does not count as harm to others; but it is hard to imagine that any political community could offer more in the way of individual discretion and prerogative than the one Rousseau described. As for the Lawgiver, who shapes citizens into 'part of a larger whole', this merely supplies the conditions under which people will perform their obligations as citizens instead of acting as 'free riders' who accept the benefits of political society without the costs. All liberal theories face the challenge of how to protect individual rights while simultaneously ensuring that people acquire civic virtue. Rousseau's theory left as much scope and protection for individual liberty as any plausible political philosophy could.

In any case, his defence of individual liberty and democracy, which held that even the English parliamentary system was tyrannical, met with great resistance in France and even in Geneva. His home city was then in the midst of a constitutional struggle between popular and aristocratic factions, and his work did much to fan the controversy. Furthermore, the theory of civil religion outraged the authorities in both places. The reasons for Rousseau's condemnation in France were more obvious given his argument that Catholicism should be outlawed. But Geneva found cause for complaint, too, first because the broad religious toleration that Rousseau defended was contrary to the Calvinist orthodoxy maintained in that city, but more importantly because he had raised doubts about the value of formal Christianity as such. He offered the same argument as Niccolo Machiavelli, a man he greatly admired, had made centuries before: that Christianity is a bad religion, politically speaking, because it makes people otherworldly and more concerned with blessedness in the next life than with freedom, equality and justice in this one. Rousseau said, 'But I am mistaken in speaking of a Christian Republic; each of these two terms excludes the other. Christianity preaches nothing but servitude and dependence. Its spirit is too favorable to tyranny for tyranny not always to profit from it. True Christians are made to be slaves; they know it and are hardly moved by it; this brief life has too little value in their eyes' (S 149). One can hardly conceive of the courage or madness required to publish such sentiments under his own name in eighteenth-century France and Geneva. A few weeks later he published the last great masterpiece that would come out in his lifetime, his didactic novel *Emile*. Together the two works made him a hunted man throughout Europe.

CHAPTER 5

EMILE

Emile is an unusual book in both form and content. It begins as a treatise on education but soon changes into a didactic and sometimes quite dramatic novel. It seems to exemplify a model educational programme, yet Rousseau mocked parents who tried to raise their children according to its plan. It claims to show the way to create a 'natural man', but goes on to prescribe a highly contrived and artificial programme of education. It begins with the statement that educators must choose whether to form men or citizens because they cannot do both, yet leaves it unclear which one of them the character Emile is supposed to be. And while it was widely read and also condemned in Rousseau's own time, its most controversial passages were not to do with education but religion, which he discussed only in a digression from the main line of argument.

Its subsequent influence has been equally ambivalent. The great thinkers of the generation immediately after Rousseau, especially Kant, thought that it was one of the most important philosophical works ever written. Yet it is hardly read by philosophers today, while *The Social Contract*, which Rousseau regarded as an unfinished philosophical fragment, is endlessly mined for insights and arguments. Part of the reason that *Emile* is largely ignored today is that the only accepted literary genre for philosophical writing is thought to be the thesis-driven article or book. This tends to make philosophers uncomfortable in dealing with other modes of expression, and quite awkward in handling them. An exception is of course made for Plato's dialogues, but even they are often treated as if they were really thesis-driven essays struggling to shake off their literary form. This modern prejudice does much to shape the perceived philosophical canon, with the result that minor works such as Leibniz's

'Discourse on Metaphysics' are considered to be important while undoubted masterpieces such as Hume's *History of England* and Rousseau's *Emile* are hardly read by philosophers. Rousseau himself believed that *Emile* was 'the best and most important' of all his writings, and it is hard to disagree (C 529–30).

BACKGROUND

Emile gave the most full and polished expression to Rousseau's essential thesis of 'the natural goodness of man'. To see how this is so, it is especially useful to recall his second 'Discourse', to which *Emile* is deeply connected. His goal in that essay had been to reconcile the theory of the natural goodness of man with the obvious fact that many people are immoral. To answer this, he constructed a hypothetical history of human life on earth as an abstraction, or idealization, showing how humanity's innate goodness might be shaped by circumstances into something cruel and harmful. The 'Discourse' began with 'natural man' and showed how 'the changes that occurred in his constitution, the progress he has made, and the knowledge he has acquired' affected his original nature (D 197).

The purpose of *Emile* was similar in the sense that it was intended to address the same topic but from a different direction. In a private letter written shortly after the novel's publication, Rousseau denied that it was really a book about education. 'You say quite correctly that it is impossible to produce an Emile. But I cannot believe that you take the book that carries this name for a true treatise on education. It is a rather philosophic work on the principle, advanced by the author in other writings, *that man is naturally good*. To reconcile this principle with that other no less certain truth that men are wicked, it was necessary to show the origin of all the vices in the history of the human heart.' And in his 'Letter to Beaumont' written in the same period he further explained, 'I showed that all the vices which are imparted to the human heart are not natural to it; I showed how they came to be acquired; I followed, so to speak, their genealogy, and revealed how by the successive corruption of men's original goodness, they became what they are now' (N 278). The epigraph to *Emile* is, as always, very telling. It comes from the Roman philosopher Seneca. 'We are sick with evils that can be cured; and nature, having brought us forth sound, itself helps us if we wish to be improved.'

The difference between the second 'Discourse' and *Emile* is in scale. Both describe a process of change and development in human character, yet the 'Discourse' explains it in terms of humanity in general while *Emile* looks at the development of a single young man. In fact, the stages of Emile's education in some ways mirror the stages of humanity in the second 'Discourse'. Thus the relationship between the two works is roughly the same as that between the sciences of evolutionary biology on the one hand and embryology on the other. One explains things by looking at the origin of the whole species while the other explains the same things by looking at the development of individuals. The obvious methodological difference between these sciences and Rousseau's theory is that he granted his evolutionary account was merely conjectural and that his individual, Emile, was fictional.

As for the occasion of the work, it appears that he began writing it in 1759, yet the circumstances are unclear. In his autobiographies and letters, he said very little about the source and motivation of *Emile*, which is unusual given that even in the case of his minor essays he usually gave evidence about when and why they were produced. Some have suggested that he wrote *Emile* in response to friends who asked him for advice about how to raise their children. Indeed, this is the framing device that he used in the Preface, which begins, 'This collection of reflections and observation, disordered and almost incoherent, was begun to gratify a good mother who knows how to think' (E 33). Yet this thesis is tenuous. As mentioned in the first chapter, Rousseau seems to have abandoned all of his children to orphanages, so there is little reason to believe that his associates would have considered him an expert on child rearing. Furthermore, his comments in the Preface cannot be read at face value. For example, it is clear from external evidence that he believed *Emile* to be his best book, so the veracity of the Preface, with its self-deprecating tone, is suspect from the first line.

One must also recall that the book is not actually about how to raise children. It has the more abstract and philosophical purpose of showing how the thesis of the natural goodness of man can be reconciled with the undeniable immorality of many or most people, which is to say that it presents a theory of human nature and society. Rousseau had been working on this issue since he first saw the essay question proposed by the Dijon Academy in 1749, so it is not surprising to see him develop it further in the period that saw the apex of his creative and philosophical powers. Moreover, he had been interested in education since his time working as a tutor to the Mably family in Dijon, in the context of which he had even written a short treatise in 1740 called 'Project for the education of M. de Sainte-Marie'. Furthermore, he began *Emile* immediately after finishing his epistolary novel *Julie* so it is understandable that he might find it comfortable to continue writing in narrative mode, especially given that his subject was, in his words, the history of a human heart (C 478).

The stated purpose of the book is to show how a proper education might succeed in forming a young man who is both happy and virtuous, but it had the larger purpose of defending the thesis that people are naturally good and that they are made bad and unhappy by society. It begins as a treatise on educational theory, but soon evolves, in the first chapter, into a didactic novel, which tells the story of the boyhood and education of a young man named Emile and his tutor Jean-Jacques, who is more or less Rousseau himself. The design of the work, which is divided into five books, follows Rousseau's analysis of the development of human character. It begins with the ringing and by now familiar sentiment, 'Everything is good as it leaves the hands of the Author of things; everything degenerates in the hands of man' (E 37).

This is a restatement of Rousseau's view that human problems are caused by human institutions rather than by something in the natural world or an inevitable defect in human nature itself. People are made bad and unhappy by institutions. And, again, the root of his social thought is the rejection both of the Christian theory of original sin and of Hobbes's theory that people are naturally selfish and vain. Thus the book goes on to describe an 'education according to nature', the point of which is to cultivate Emile's natural goodness. The core of this educational theory is to 'Observe nature and follow the path it maps out for you' (E 47). And its goal is to shape or form a person who is not only happy, but who is also 'good for himself and good for others' (E 41).

In some ways the education that Rousseau recommended should be easy to understand, because its essence is to let Emile be himself. The teacher need only get out of the way of nature. Rousseau said, 'To form this rare man, what do we have to do . . . What must be done is to prevent anything from being done' (E 41). He went on to say, however, that it is not as easy as it sounds, because many of the institutions that would surround anyone in the present time are already corrupt. So to educate him according to nature requires that the parents and tutor create a highly artificial environment. They must shelter Emile from the social, political and economic forces that make people immoral and unhappy. It may seem paradoxical to say that a natural education requires an artificial environment, so to explain this point Rousseau developed an elaborate but helpful metaphor.

He began by comparing people as they exist today to highly trained shrubs, such as the espaliered plants that one finds in French gardens. He argued that these are unnatural products of human fancy, the proof of which is that as soon as the chance comes they revert to their original growth habits. He said that a typical person today 'wants nothing as nature made it, not even man; for him man must be trained like a school horse; man must be fashioned in keeping with his fancy like a tree in his garden' (E 37). Yet if people were not twisted to fit into modern institutions, things would be even worse. 'In the present state of things a man abandoned to himself in the midst of other men from birth would be the most disfigured of all. Prejudices, authority, necessity, example, all the social institutions in which we find ourselves submerged would stifle nature in him and put nothing in its place. Nature there would be like a shrub that chance had caused to be born in the middle of a path and that the passers-by soon cause to perish by bumping into it from all sides and bending it in every direction' (E 37).

In other words, while present educational arrangements twist and deform human nature, the surrounding environment is so corrupt that people would be worse off if they were not moulded to fit it. So, Rousseau asked, continuing with the metaphor, how can one hope to grow a shrub that is natural when merely to leave it alone in a polluted environment would be to ruin it? The solution is to create an artificially natural environment by walling it off from the outside world. 'It is to you that I address myself, tender and foresighted mother, who are capable of keeping the nascent shrub away from the highway and securing it from the impact of human opinions! Cultivate and water the young plant before it dies. Its fruits will one day be your delights. Form an enclosure around your child's soul at an early date' (E 37–8).

While most of the specific arguments in the five books of *Emile* are easier to understand than those found in the 'Discourses' and

The Social Contract, the overall method of the work may appear somewhat puzzling. For it is unclear how it reconciles Rousseau's theory of 'the natural goodness of man' with the actual wickedness of many people. After all, Emile's education is successful in the sense that, by the end of the book, he has achieved some degree of wisdom, goodness and happiness. So the reader is left to wonder in what sense the work shows 'the origin of all the vices in the history of the human heart' as Rousseau said it did. The answer is that in showing an education according to nature, Rousseau indicated all the places where it could have gone wrong, and typically does go wrong in modern civilization. Indeed, much of the argument is taken up not with his own proposals but with criticism of common practices, which he regarded as the source of unhappiness and vice. For example, in the first pages of the book he argued that Emile's own parents, not nannies and nurses, should raise him, and that he should be breast-fed by his own mother. He then goes on to explain why the practices of the French upper classes, who often hardly saw their offspring, were bad for children's character (E 44).

Yet there is a deeper paradox in the way that Rousseau framed his argument, and this one is more difficult to resolve. Recall that one important part of Rousseau's political theory in *The Social Contract* was the 'Lawgiver'. This is the figure or institution that shapes people into citizens or at least into potential citizens. Rousseau argued that this figure is necessary, because people are naturally quite individualistic. And while they have no desire to harm others, they also have no natural instinct to sacrifice themselves for others, as citizenship requires. This was his point in the passage cited in the previous chapter. 'Anyone who dares to institute a people must feel capable of, so to speak, changing human nature; of transforming each individual who by himself is a perfectly solitary whole into part of a larger whole from which the individual would as it were receive his life and his being' (S 69). In other words, to be a citizen one must have one's nature broken and rebuilt.

In *Emile*, Rousseau seemed to reaffirm this theory. He said, 'Forced to combat nature or the social institutions, one must choose between making a man or a citizen, for one cannot make both at the same time' (E 39). He then continued, 'Natural man is entirely for himself. He is a numerical unity, the absolute whole which is relative only to itself or its kind. Civil man is only a fractional unity dependent on the denominator; his value is determined by his relation to the whole, which is the social body. Good social institutions are those that best know how to denature man, to take his absolute existence from him in order to give him a relative one and transport the *I* into the common unity, with the result that each individual believes himself no longer one but a part of the unity and no longer feels except within the whole' (E39–40). He concluded, 'He who in civil order wants to preserve the primacy of the sentiments of nature does not know what he wants. Always in contradiction with himself, always floating between his inclinations and his duties, he will never be either man or citizen' (E 40). But this raises the obvious question of which one Emile is supposed to be. Is he educated to be a 'natural man' or a 'civil man'?

It seems that he must be a natural man, because the explicit purpose of the book is to describe an education according to nature, and the method that the tutor follows is always to 'observe nature and follow the path it maps out for you'. Plus, the secret of the education is that, 'What must be done is to prevent anything from being done'. Yet things are not that simple, because the culmination of Emile's education in Book V is that he is taught how to be a citizen and even given a condensed version of *The Social Contract* to teach him his civic duties. This has led some scholars to believe that the purpose of his education is to create a 'civil man' and even to argue that the civil society described in *The Social Contract* would be a commonwealth of people like Emile. This issue is extremely perplexing, and it is not only a question of how the two works go together; it also raises questions about the meaning of *Emile* itself. If Rousseau believed that people are naturally quite asocial, and if Emile's education is designed to cultivate his natural goodness, then in what sense can he be a citizen when on Rousseau's own theory a person must be 'denatured' in order to perform the functions of citizenship? The question has no ready answer.

Yet this may have been Rousseau's point. To see why this is so, one can look at his distinction between the educational programme developed by Plato and that of the Spartan king Lycurgus. From the time Rousseau began his first 'Discourse' in 1749, Sparta represented for him the extreme case of a perfectly designed city. Its every institution and custom was directed towards forming ideal citizens, and it offered Rousseau a bottomless mine of evidence for his twin claims that the sciences and arts erode civic virtue and that people must be broken and reformed in order to be good citizens. This was his reason for saying that Sparta was not only perfect but also 'monstrous in its perfection'. Yet he also admired many aspects of Plato's political thought, as presented in both his *Republic* and *Laws*. So in *Emile* he refined this argument by saying that while Lycurgus had 'denatured the heart of man' as a Lawgiver must, Plato's recommendations, if they had been followed, would only have 'purified' it. And it is for this reason that Rousseau called Plato's *Republic* 'the most beautiful educational treatise ever written' (E 40).

This suggests that Rousseau's opinion was more moderate than it first appeared, because it implies that people can be formed into decent and happy citizens by an education that shapes and purifies their natural instincts rather than by one that annihilates them. But he seemed willing to leave it as an open question. He said, 'To be something, to be oneself and always one, a man must act as he speaks; he must always be decisive in making his choice, make it in a lofty style, and stick to it. I am waiting to be shown this marvel so as to know whether he is a man or a citizen, or how he goes about being both at the same time' (E 40). He went on to say that although Plato's educational programme might have succeeded in forming such a person, it is no longer viable today so, 'There remains, finally, domestic education or the education of nature. But what will a man raised uniquely for himself become for others? If perchance the double object we set for ourselves could be joined in a single one by removing the contradictions of man, a great obstacle to his happiness would be removed. In order to judge of this, he would have to be seen wholly formed: his inclinations would have to be observed, his progress seen, his development followed. In a word, the natural man would have to be known. I believe that one will have made a few steps in these researches when one has read this writing' (E 41).

This then was the goal that Rousseau set for himself in writing *Emile*. He believed that people are naturally good and capable of happiness, but that modern institutions encourage vice and misery. So his first hope was to show an alternative educational programme that would cultivate the student's (Emile's) natural goodness and thereby help him to be virtuous and fulfilled. His virtue would consist in his disinclination to harm others, and his fulfilment would be found in feelings of wholeness, consistency and 'the sentiment of existence' that comes with such integrity (E 42). In developing this argument, Rousseau could also explain where modern institutions go wrong and thereby show the origin of vice and unhappiness.

But he also believed that people are naturally quite inward and unconcerned for others, at least beyond their immediate kin, which raises the question of whether a 'natural man', who was happy and benign, could also be a citizen. He left it open whether Emile, whose natural integrity would be the opposite of the citizen's brokenness, could be a good citizen too. And while the end of the book is optimistic on this last point, there are also reasons for doubt.

In its structure, the novel proceeds chronologically through Emile's infancy, boyhood, adolescence and young adult years. The first Book covers Emile's early childhood up to the age of two. The second follows him to the age of 12, describing the period from when he is first able to speak and walk on his own to the beginning of puberty. The third Book covers the shortest period, between the ages of 12 or 13 and 15, which Rousseau believed to be especially formative. The fourth Book describes Emile's adolescence, from 15 to 20. And the last Book covers Emile's final steps to independence, including his marriage and his last lessons in citizenship and the duties of adulthood, up to his mid-twenties. At each stage Rousseau defends fascinating proposals for Emile's education while offering severe objections to the common practices of his time.

THE ARGUMENT

The guiding idea of the educational programme is that the tutor must control the three forces that shape Emile's body and character, which Rousseau called 'nature, men, and things'. By the term nature he meant Emile's physiological development, which for the most part is out of the hands of the parents and tutor. They should, however, have some control over the things and especially the men who will influence him. 'The internal development of our faculties and our organs is the education of nature. The use we are taught to make of this development is the education of men. And what we acquire from our own experience about the objects which affect us is the education of things.' He soon continued, 'Now, of these three different educations, the one coming from nature is in no way in our control; that coming from things is in our control only in certain respects; that coming from men is the only one of which we are truly the masters. Even of it we are the masters only by hypothesis. For who can hope entirely to direct the speeches and the deeds of those surrounding a child?' (E 38).

Thus Emile's education consists in letting nature take its course, to the extent possible, and where he must interact with established human culture, to have the tutor very carefully regulate whom he interacts with and how. 'Thus', he said, 'the first education ought to be purely negative. It consists not at all in teaching virtue or truth but in securing the heart from vice and the mind from error' (E 93). The earliest parts of his educational programme, in Book I, are mostly steps taken against the common practices of sheltering children from danger and discomfort. Emile is not to be swaddled, and his limbs are allowed to move freely and to grow strong. He is not put in unnecessary danger or discomfort, but neither is he coddled. The main energies of the parents should go into keeping him physically vigorous and clean, although even in the latter case the temperature of his bath is gradually decreased so eventually he can wash in cold water without discomfort. The overall goal of this part of his education is that 'our children can be led back to their primitive vigour' (E 59).

From the early stages it becomes obvious that the education is not wholly negative, or rather it is negative in a particular sense. In Book II, for example, Emile is taught to read and to draw as soon as his body and mind are sufficiently developed. This point is important, because it shows that Rousseau's 'education according to nature' still allows Emile to be brought into a literate culture. He is gradually and carefully taught a language, taught to be clean, taught how to use eating utensils, and so on. Yet this does raise the question of how negative the negative education really is. Rousseau explained his view more fully in his 'Letter to Beaumont'. 'What I call positive education is that which tends to educate the mind beyond its age and to give the child knowledge of the duties of man. What I call negative education is that which tends to perfect the [sense] organs which are the instruments of our knowledge before giving us knowledge itself and which prepares us for reason by exercising our senses. Negative education is not lazy, far from it. It does not give us virtues but it prevents vices; it does not teach truth but preserves us from error.' From this insight come many of the ingenious and curious policies in Emile's early education. For example, as he learns to talk he is never allowed to hear words that he cannot pronounce and whose meaning he could not easily understand (E 74). Rousseau's idea was that by letting everything develop at its own speed according to its own nature Emile can preserve his integrity and virtue.

The most interesting part of the early educational programme is the way in which the tutor manages Emile's desires. In his second 'Discourse' Rousseau had argued that the greatest cause of conflict between people is *amour-propre*, or vanity. When people wish to be envied, it becomes advantageous for them to see other people do poorly. This fact causes people to wish to dominate and harm others, or at least not to help them. Much of Emile's education, therefore, is designed to shape his growing sense of self. The key theme in Emile's early education is that the tutor never allows himself to get into a battle of wills with Emile. Every impediment that the tutor raises to Emile's desires is made to seem inevitable, like a force of nature, so that Emile never develops a sense of resentment against the tutor. Rousseau's insight was that people never feel resentful about things that they think are necessary; they feel resentful only when they believe that another person is purposely preventing them from getting what they want. No one resents the force of gravity.

This aspect of his education is evident even in Book I, before Emile has a meaningful sense of self and others, and while he is still in the care of his parents or a nurse. The most obvious occasion is when he cries even though he is not in physical pain. Rousseau said, 'The lengthy tears of a child who is neither bound nor sick, who is allowed to want for nothing, are only the tears of habit and obstinacy. They are the work not of nature but of the nurse who, not knowing how to endure the importunity, multiplies it without dreaming that in making the child to keep quiet today one is encouraging him to cry more tomorrow.' He then proposed the clever solution that, 'a sure means of preventing them from continuing is to distract them by some pleasant and striking object which makes them forget that they wanted to cry. . . But it is of the most extreme importance that the child not perceive the intention to distract him, and that he enjoy himself without believing that one is thinking of him' (E 69). The point is that if the child realizes that he can change the nurse's behaviour by crying, then the battle of wills has begun.

In Book I, Rousseau gave another interesting example of how the nurse or parents could accidentally inflame the child's vanity. The example again concerns the use of language, which was a topic of great interest to Rousseau. The more obvious danger, discussed above, is that by learning too many big words the child's character will be deformed by reaching out to ideas and emotions that it is in no way ready to grasp. One can also guess that Rousseau rejected the idea that children should be taught classical languages early on. Yet he had interesting ideas about how the child's native language should be taught. He argued that enunciation should be taught simply by having the children stay outdoors most of the time, where they will not only build their physical strength but also need to speak loudly and clearly to be understood. But what should be done with a child who develops poor diction anyway? Rousseau argued that endlessly to correct him would build up resentment and vanity, so the best solution is simply to pretend, politely, that one cannot understand him (E 73).

In the end, the tutor takes this lesson to an extreme, but one that follows necessarily from Rousseau's premises.

> Let his haughty head at an early date feel the harsh yoke which nature imposes on man, the heavy yoke of necessity under which every finite being must bend. Let him see this necessity in things, never in the caprice of men. Let the bridle that restrains him be force and not authority. Do not forbid him to do that from which he should abstain; prevent him from doing it without explanations, without reasonings. What you grant him, grant at his first word, without solicitations, without prayers – above all without conditions. Grant with pleasure; refuse only with repugnance. But let all your refusals be irrevocable; let no importunity shake you; let 'no', once pronounced, be a wall of bronze against which the child will have to exhaust his strength at most five or six times in order to abandon any further attempts to overturn it (E 91).

The most extraordinary example of this kind of pedagogy comes shortly afterwards in Book II, when the tutor sees that Emile is ready to learn that he should respect other people's possessions. Rousseau said, 'I hold it to be impossible to bring a child along to the age of twelve in the bosom of society without giving him some idea of the relations of man to man and the morality of human actions. It is enough if one takes pains to ensure that the notions become necessary to him as late as possible and, when their presentation is unavoidable, to limit them to immediate utility, with the sole intention of believing himself master of everything and from doing harm to others without scruple and without knowing it' (E 97). To teach Emile this lesson the tutor and their gardener, Robert, construct an elaborate scene behind his back. Emile has seen people ploughing fields and decides that he wants to plant some beans of his own.

The tutor lets him, and each day they carefully water and cultivate the seeds. Emile is overjoyed when the seeds start to grow. Then one day they come to work the field and discover that the plants have been torn up. Emile is deeply grieved and complains to Robert, who replies that he had already planted melons in that field and that he pulled up the beans because they had ruined his crop. The tutor apologizes and gets Emile to see that it was wrong to harm someone else's possessions just as he felt wronged when his beans were damaged. Emile agrees and, in the end, Robert gives Emile a small patch of garden on the condition that he gives him half of the produce.

The tutor continues to follow the negative path even when it comes to teaching mathematics and the natural sciences. Certainly Emile cannot learn something so complicated merely by being left alone, and yet the educational programme has a negative purpose even in teaching positive lessons in the sciences. Rousseau said, 'Remember always that the spirit of my education consists not in teaching the child many things, but in never letting anything but accurate and clear ideas enter his brain. Were he to know nothing it would be of little importance to me provided he made no mistakes. I put truth in his head only to guard him against the errors he would learn in their place. Reason and judgment come slowly; prejudices come in crowds; it is from them that he must be preserved' (E 171). Here he again presented his view that imagination, sentiment and prejudice harm people by encouraging false beliefs and vanity. Emile's education is designed to protect him from these more than to give him a store of words, ideas, facts and theories. It is designed to help his organs and bodily senses work correctly and his knowledge comes less from books than from carefully experiencing the world through all his senses.

Book III begins when Emile is 12 or 13. At this time he starts to grow very rapidly in physical strength and he is capable of exercising some judgement of his own. According to the tutor, this period is unique in Emile's life because it is the one time that his strength exceeds his desires. Both as a young child and as an adult, the danger is that his desires will outstrip his powers; but as an early adolescent, whose body is growing quickly but who does not yet have complicated adult ideas and emotions, he can do more than he wants. This puts the educational programme on a new and unusual footing. 'Although this interval during which the individual is capable of more than he desires is not the time of his greatest absolute strength, it is, as I have said, the time of his greatest relative strength. It is the most precious time of life, a time which comes only once, a very short time, one even shorter – as will be seen in what follows – because of the importance of using it well' (E 166). Thus Rousseau devoted all of Book III to only two years of Emile's life.

One of the most interesting aspects of this period is that Emile is given his first book. The choice says a very great deal about the meaning of *Emile*, for he is given neither the Bible nor a classic of ancient literature, but rather a copy of Daniel Defoe's *Robinson Crusoe*. While scholars debate the precise meaning of this choice, a few points are clear. First, one must notice that he was not given the works of Plutarch, particularly his *Lives*, which was the work that most influenced Rousseau and which he believed had a generally beneficial influence on his character. That work concerns the heroes of the Greek city-states and republican Rome who sought glory in self-sacrifice and public service, all of which are still unknown to Emile. Because Crusoe is abandoned on what he takes to be a desert island, he is completely freed from the opinions of others. All of his thoughts and actions are dedicated to the practical problems of how to supply real necessities. He has, in a sense, become freed from the powers of vanity, envy and greed, with the result that he can genuinely think for himself about what is important and how to get it. Emile finds in this book a mirror of his own nascent feelings, and a model of resourcefulness, without any reference to human society, politics, pride, envy, God, the afterlife and the other ideas that Rousseau believed do much to corrupt the human character if presented too early in life.

This is also the moment at which Emile's education is most unlike Rousseau's. Rousseau spent his first ten years immersed in literature, first in a series of French romance novels and then the classics of Greek and Roman antiquity. These works cultivated in him a series of thoughts and feelings that were inappropriate to his age and from which he never really recovered. As mentioned before, he said of his youthful reading, 'In a short time I acquired by this dangerous method, not only an extreme facility in reading and expressing myself, but a singular insight for my age into the passions. I had no idea of the facts, but I was already familiar with every feeling. I had grasped nothing; I had sensed everything' (C 20). Partly from this influence came his own feelings of vanity and his sentimentality, which he believed to be the source of his own unhappiness and which caused him to refer to himself as someone 'whose passions have forever destroyed their original simplicity' (D 203).

However, the crucial transition in Book III is not that Emile reads his first novel, but that his relationship to his tutor changes. In the earlier books, although the tutor had complete control over everything that Emile saw and did, the authority was completely hidden. Emile's life was an elaborately managed stage production in which the tutor appeared merely as his playmate. In Book III, when Emile's intellectual faculties have grown, his relationship to the tutor becomes more honest. This is perhaps the most difficult part of his education, because the tutor must demonstrate his authority without causing resentment in Emile or inflaming his vanity. The tutor succeeds largely by meeting Emile on his own terms and by taking advantage of the qualities that he cultivated in Emile while he was still his playmate.

The new activities designed by the tutor are intended to engage his existing needs and interests. Emile has very few desires in any case, and most of those are easily satisfied, so he has no reason to defy the tutor. Emile also begins to study the natural sciences more deeply, although, as one would expect, the tutor's method is not to have Emile read books but rather to have him build things and observe the natural world directly. Emile develops his mind and body by practice rather than precept, and he continues to learn about morality through interacting with people and nature rather than through formal lessons. Because Emile's imagination is not overly active, he does not picture himself in a different situation than the one he is in, and thus has no reason to change it. Furthermore, his intellect is quite mature, so he realizes both that the tutor is much smarter than he is, and that he would be unable to succeed on his own.

The effect of these further lessons is to sharpen Emile's mind. By the end of Book III, when he is 15, his intellect is largely mature. He knows quite little, yet he has avoided the intellectual diseases of superstition, fanaticism and excessive imagination. In a passage that echoes Plato's *Apology*, Rousseau says, 'Emile has little knowledge, but what he has is truly his own. He knows nothing halfway. Among the small number of things he knows and knows well, the most important is that there are many things of which he is ignorant and which he can know one day. . . Emile has a mind that is universal not by its learning but by its faculty to acquire learning; a mind that is open, intelligent, and ready for everything' (E 207). Yet while his mind is remarkably mature, his emotional life is still quite simple. He is benign and has no inclination to harm others, but his emotions and his moral precepts are limited. Because he has been taught to live only for himself, he is pleasant, tough and generally kind, but nothing more.

Rousseau describes him thus, 'Emile is laborious, temperate, patient, firm, and full of courage. His imagination is in no way inflamed and never enlarges dangers. He is sensitive to few ills, and he knows constancy in endurance because he has not yet learned to quarrel with destiny.' Yet, 'He considers himself without regard to others and finds it good that others do not think of him. He demands nothing of anyone and believes he owes nothing to anyone. He is alone in human society; he counts on himself alone' (E 208). What he lacks is an emotional life, but this will inevitably come as he continues to mature. Thus, Rousseau said that the next step in the growth of his character is the development of romantic passion and his sense of *amour-propre*, 'the first and most natural of all the passions' (E 208). 'Now,' he says, 'our child, ready to stop being a child, has become aware of himself as an individual. Now he senses more than ever the necessity which attaches him to things. After having begun by exercising his body and his senses, we have exercised his mind and judgment. Finally we have joined the use of his limbs to that of his faculties. We have made an active and thinking being. It remains for us, in order to complete the man, only to make a loving and feeling being – that is to say, to perfect reason by sentiment' (E 203).

To widen the scope of Emile's interests, the tutor takes advantage of Emile's natural sense of pity. As in his second 'Discourse', Rousseau argues that people naturally feel pain at the suffering of others, from which it follows that Emile's sympathy can be broadened by acquainting him with those who are in need. Yet the tutor is careful not to expose him to too much suffering lest he become indifferent to others. In fact, exposing Emile to people who are sick and poor serves a double purpose. It begins to develop his emotional capacities, and it also shapes his sense of *amour-propre*, or vanity, in beneficial ways. Rousseau argued that it is inevitable that Emile will compare himself and his condition to others. If he finds them better off than he is, it might inflame his envy and his desire to see others so poorly. But if his first contacts are limited to the poor and infirm, he is likely to feel both happy with his own condition and sorry for theirs. At this point the tutor also gives Emile history books to read, especially Plutarch. This is intended to widen further the scope of his concern, but it also seems that if Emile meets people who are his superiors for the first time in a book rather than real life, the effect will be less shocking.

These three developments are tied together tightly in Rousseau's presentation. Emile's emerging sense of vanity, his sexual maturity and his participation in the social world develop together and interact in many complicated ways, which the tutor does his best to guide and manage. It is no wonder that Book IV is the longest and most difficult chapter of the work. Indeed, the chance that any one of these factors could go wrong and destroy all that the tutor has built is so great that it seems to challenge Rousseau's theory of 'the natural goodness of man'. For where is the goodness in a being whose passions are so likely to make him cruel and destructive? Rousseau himself said, 'As the roaring of the sea precedes a tempest from afar this stormy revolution is proclaimed by the murmur of the nascent passions. A mute fermentation warns of danger's approach. A change in humor, frequent anger, a mind in constant agitation, make the child almost unmanageable. He becomes deaf to the voice which made him docile. His feverishness turns him into a lion. He disregards his guide; he no longer wishes to be governed' (E 211).

Rousseau responded to these questions by offering an even more fine-grained analysis of vanity than he gave in his second 'Discourse'. He said, 'The source of our passions, the origin and the principle of all the others, the only one born with man and which never leaves him so long as he lives is self love [*amour de soi*] – a primitive, innate passion, which is anterior to every other, and of which all others are in a sense modifications. In this sense all passions are natural.' In other words, the concern for one's own life and well-being is at the root of all human psychological dispositions. And while it can be highly modified by circumstance, 'most of these modifications have alien causes without which they would never have come to pass; and these same modifications, far from being advantageous to us, are harmful' (E 212–13). The primary cause of these modifications is interaction with other people when the parties compare their relative merits and well-being. 'Self-love, which regards only ourselves, is contented when our true needs are satisfied. But *amour-propre*, which makes comparisons, is never content and never could be, because this sentiment, preferring ourselves to others, also demands others to prefer us to themselves, which is impossible. This is how the gentle and affectionate passions are born of self-love, and how the hateful and irascible passions are born of *amour-propre'* (E 213–14).

Thus, the solution, as much as there is one, is to help Emile to be happy and confident with himself, while always aware of the suffering of others. Knowing their difficulties helps him to feel more satisfied with his lot and while, on Rousseau's analysis, vanity can never be eradicated from his character, it can be directed towards beneficial channels. Emile feels confident in his mental and physical abilities and he desires almost nothing that he does not already have. His imagination has been kept under control, so he is pleased with the world that surrounds him. This line of thought leads Rousseau to another interesting aspect of his education programme, namely that the tutor contrives to slow down Emile's emotional (and especially sexual) development, so that he has time to incorporate these new feelings into his already solid character. 'This is one of the most frequent abuses committed by the philosophy of our age. Nature's instruction is late and slow; men's is almost always premature. In the former case the senses wake the imagination; in the latter the imagination wakes the senses; it gives them a precocious activity which cannot fail to enervate and weaken individuals first and in the long run the species itself' (E 215).

Again, by letting Emile's body and his reason develop before his imagination and emotions, the tutor is able to make him strong, confident and happy in his circumstances before introducing him to women and social life. This is the pervasive theme of *Emile*, and especially of Book IV, where the key to controlling Emile's growing vanity and sexual drive is to let them develop from his own good character rather than forcing them upon him. Rousseau argued that when a child is given adult words, images and ideas before he has adult reason and emotions, it 'gives a precocious fermentation to his blood. He knows what the object of his desire ought to be before he even experiences them. It is not nature which excites him; it is he who forces nature. It has nothing more to teach him in making him man. He was one in thought a long time before he was one in fact'. Whereas if he were allowed to mature at his own rate, 'A long restlessness precedes the first desires; a long ignorance puts them off the track. One desires without knowing what. . . One begins to take an interest in those surrounding us; one begins to feel that one is not made to live alone. It is thus that the heart is opened to the human affections and becomes capable of attachment' (E 220). The tutor introduces Emile to sexual life and social responsibility by waiting until his late teens, when Emile genuinely feels the desire for them, and knows what he desires. This keeps Emile's character moderate and patient and prevents the development of destructive vanity.

Meanwhile, Emile's intellectual development progresses from the study of nature to the highest objects of all, religion and 'the Author of nature'. One can see why religion had no role in Emile's education up to this time. The essence of the educational programme was that he is never to be given words, ideas or objects that he cannot understand, which obviously implies that a religious catechism could not be part of his education, especially if the religion in question were one so full of mystery and paradox as Christianity. Rousseau said, 'I foresee how many readers will be surprised at seeing me trace the whole first ages of my pupil without speaking to him of religion. At fifteen he did not know whether he had a soul. And perhaps at eighteen it is not yet time for him to learn it; for if he learns it sooner than he ought, he runs the risk of never knowing it' (E 257). While the passage in Book IV where the tutor introduces Emile to religion is a small part of the whole work, it is interesting in itself and had very great consequences for Rousseau after it was published. As one would expect, the tutor waits to introduce theology until Emile himself asks questions about the ultimate nature of things. Then the tutor gives him the famous 'Profession of Faith of the Savoyard Vicar'. Here the narrative becomes quite complicated.

The 'Profession of Faith' was written by Rousseau, of course, but in the novel he has the tutor, who is in a sense Rousseau himself, give the pamphlet to Emile, saying that it was written by a priest from Savoy. Now, in the context of *Emile*, this is true. The tutor, Jean-Jacques, did not write the pamphlet; it was actually written by the priest, except that (in real life) the priest is a fictional character created by Rousseau, and the 'Profession' was actually written by Rousseau himself. Rousseau then inserted the whole text of the 'Profession' into *Emile*. Furthermore, in the novel, the 'Profession' is itself embedded in a longer document that the narrator presents to the reader as having been written by a fourth person, who is neither Rousseau, nor the tutor, nor the priest. And to complete the confusion, this document is a first-person narrative that basically follows the contours of Rousseau's own early life while he was in Turin.

Although the narrative trappings are complicated, the inner message is quite clear. The priest from Savoy advocates a modest natural religion that suits Emile's education perfectly, because it relies on nothing more than Emile's strong reason and good character. The vicar argues that the scope of human reason is very narrow and that we cannot hope to understand the ultimate causes of the way things are. We gain knowledge from experience; yet our experience is extremely small even when augmented by scientific instruments. The best route is to trust our judgement and experience and to expect no more than that. 'Therefore, taking the love of truth as my whole philosophy, and as my whole method an easy and simple rule that exempts me from the vain subtlety of arguments, I pick up again on the basis of this rule the examination of the knowledge that interests me. I am resolved to accept as evident all knowledge to which in the sincerity of my heart I cannot refuse my consent; to accept as true all which appears to have a necessary connection with this first knowledge; and to leave all the rest in uncertainty without rejecting it or accepting it and without tormenting myself to clarify it if it leads to nothing useful for practice' (E 269–70).

The vicar follows with a brief account of his theories regarding the physical and psychological world, and eventually of the deity. His belief in God is based on a simple version of the teleological argument. The universe shows order and design, which presupposes a supreme intelligence and power to put the whole into motion. So the vicar infers 'that the world is governed by a powerful and wise will. I see it or, rather, I sense it; and that is something important for me to know. But is this same world eternal or created? Is there a single principle of things? Or, are there two or many of them, and what is their nature? I know nothing about all this, and what does it matter to me? As soon as this knowledge has something to do with my interests, I shall make an effort to acquire it. Until then I renounce idle questions which may agitate my *amour-propre* but are useless for my conduct and are beyond my reason' (E 276–77). The result, obviously, is a kind of spirituality that is minimal, sceptical, naturalistic, moderate, tolerant and informal.

The 'Profession' contains a series of further interesting arguments about religion and society. Based on his beliefs about the limits of human reason, the vicar goes on to criticize all forms of fanaticism and intolerance, especially that of Christians against non-Christians. 'At Constantinople the Turks state their arguments, but we do not dare to state our own. There it is our turn to crawl. If the Turks demand from us the same respect for Mohammed that we demand for Jesus Christ from the Jews, who do not believe in him any more than we believe in Mohammed, are the Turks wrong? Are we right? According to what equitable principle shall we solve this question?' He continues, 'And if the son of a Christian does well in following his father's religion without a profound and impartial examination, why would the son of a Turk do wrong in similarly following his father's religion? I defy all the intolerant people in the world to answer this question in a manner satisfactory to a sensible man' (E 304–6). The vicar also goes on to argue against the belief in miracles and against organized religion generally, because they encourage superstition, ignorance and subservience. And he reiterates that the ideas of original sin and that one can only be saved within the Church violate the principle that God is just. 'Pressed by these arguments, some would prefer to make God unjust and to punish the innocent for their father's sin rather than to renounce their barbarous dogma' (E 306).

Because the 'Profession' is folded into such a complicated narrative structure, it is difficult to know how far it is intended to convey Rousseau's own beliefs. Certainly much of it is consistent with his other letters and published works, especially his views on human knowledge, religious toleration and original sin. Yet many commentators have noted that the 'Profession' also contains a kind of dualism between body and soul, and between good and evil in human nature, which is uncharacteristic of Rousseau's other works. Another possibility is that Rousseau hid himself in the text because the views expressed were controversial, as indeed they were. The 'Profession' attacked dogmatism, the belief in miracles, superstition, the divinity of Christ, religious intolerance and organized religion as such.

And yet it is hard to believe that Rousseau intended to hide his views, because many of the things he spoke in his own voice were just as incendiary as what he put in the mouth of the vicar. His cutting tone is sometimes extraordinary when one thinks of the charged circumstances in which he was writing. For example, in defending his view that children should only be taught what they are able to understand, he said, 'If I had to depict sorry stupidity, I would depict a pedant teaching the catechism to children. If I wanted to make a child go mad, I would oblige him to explain what he says in saying his catechism. . . Doubtless there is not a moment to lose in order to merit eternal salvation. But if in order to obtain it, it is enough to repeat certain words, I do not see what prevents us from peopling heaven with starlings and magpies just as well as with children' (E 257).

Eventually, at the end of Book IV, the tutor sends Emile into the wider world. He travels to a fashionable city (a fictionalized Paris) to become acquainted with the different kinds of people there along with their customs and manners. Emile's natural politeness and courtesy, along with his clear mind, allow him to be accepted into sophisticated society without being corrupted by it. The city provides him with a final polish and worldliness necessary for his future success. This is another point at which it becomes clear that Rousseau did not prize ignorance and mere rusticity, as some of his critics have claimed. Indeed, Emile acquires a very sophisticated higher education. His taste in art is cultivated and refined, his moral judgements are made more subtle, he learns the classics of ancient literature, his manners become sophisticated and he learns to write well. Yet all of this is performed in the name of decency and public service. Rousseau said, for example, 'Knowledge of what can be agreeable or disagreeable to men is necessary not only to someone who needs men but also to someone who wishes to be useful to them. It is even important to please them in order to serve them, and the art of writing is far from an idle study when one uses it to make the truth heard' (E 341). This is consistent with his discussion of high culture in the 'Discourse on the Sciences and Arts' and puts the argument of that work in proper perspective.

Even though Emile is now 20, the tutor still manipulates almost every event and encounter. The occasion of his marriage is especially interesting, or perhaps egregious. Before Emile goes to the city, where he could easily be corrupted, the tutor has him imagine a perfect wife for himself. The woman should not be completely perfect in the abstract sense, but she should be the perfect match for Emile and for the life he intends to live. So Emile and the tutor conjure up a vivid image of such a woman and, at the tutor's suggestion, they name her Sophie. Then the tutor drops a hint that such a person might already exist, but he leaves some doubt as Emile goes to the city. His idea is that this image of future virtue and love will prevent Emile from falling into the debauches of the city. In fact, the tutor had found him a prospective wife long ago, and her name, of course, is Sophie. The whole enterprise was a ruse to save him from the dangers of the city and to make him fall in love all the more fully when he finally meets the woman and it happens that she has the same personality, demeanour and name as his imagined ideal.

Book V of *Emile* depicts the end of the educational programme as Emile gets married and takes on the duties of citizenship. It also contains a famous and infamous summary of a parallel education programme for girls, in which Sophie takes the place of Emile. Rousseau discussed many of the same themes as he did in Emile's education and he showed great care for and interest in Sophie. Again, the essence of her education is that everything should be done according to nature. The growth of Sophie's body and mind lead the way and her environment follows. Her imagination is narrowed while her intellect and judgement grow. Yet while her educational programme is in every way as sophisticated as Emile's, there is no doubt that Rousseau was a male chauvinist, although not a misogynist. For while the purpose of her education, like Emile's, is to allow her to perfect her nature, the perfection of her nature is to serve a man. 'In the union of the sexes each contributes equally to the common aim, but not in the same way. From this diversity arises the first assignable difference in the moral relations of the two sexes. One ought to be active and strong, the other passive and weak. One must necessarily will and be able; it suffices that the other put up little resistance' (E 358).

One might think that from such a view would follow an educational programme that ensures that women are pliant and ignorant. Yet his proposals are somewhat more complicated than that. It is true that he said, 'the whole education of women ought to relate to men. To please men, to be useful to them, to make herself loved and honored by them, to raise them when young, to care for them when grown, to counsel them, to console them, to make their lives agreeable and sweet – these are the duties of women at all times' (E 365). Yet he argued that these offices require exceptional training of mind and body.

> Does it follow that she ought to be raised in ignorance of everything and limited to the housekeeping functions alone? Will a man turn his companion into his servant? Will he deprive himself of the greatest charm of society with her? In order to make her more subject, will he prevent her from feeling anything, from knowing anything? Will he make her into a

veritable automaton? Surely not. It is not thus that nature has spoken in giving women such agreeable and nimble minds. On the contrary, nature wants them to think, to judge, to love, to know, to cultivate their minds as well as their looks (E 364).

Thus, the situation is more complicated than it appears at the start. The subordination of women that he recommends is of a particular kind that also requires them to be highly educated. The issue becomes especially confusing in light of Rousseau's idea that the best women are, in fact, completely in control of their men. 'But the woman who is at once decent, lovable, self-controlled, who forces those about her to respect her, who has reserve and modesty, who, in a word, sustains love by means of esteem, sends her lovers with a nod to the end of the world, to combat, to glory, to death, to anything she pleases. This seems to me to be a noble empire, and one well worth the price of its purchase' (E 393). And he concludes his discussion of Sophie's education by saying that, 'there is nothing that cannot be obtained under nature's direction from women as well as from men' (E 405).

There follows an elaborate ruse in which Emile and Sophie are introduced, fall in love, and are allowed to court. Before they are married, however, something interesting happens. The tutor says that even for his 20-plus years of effort, Emile's education is not complete. He has a strong intellect and a good character, he knows himself and his basic moral obligations to others, but he is ignorant about politics and political duty. Rousseau said, 'Now that Emile has considered himself in his physical relations with other beings and in his moral relations with other men, it remains for him to consider himself in his civil relations with his fellow citizens. To do that, he must begin by studying the nature of government in general, the diverse forms of government, and finally the particular government under which he was born, so that he may find out whether it suits him to live there' (E 455).

To teach him the principles of political philosophy the tutor gives him a shortened version of *The Social Contract*, and to learn about politics in detail he embarks on a two-year tour of Europe's capitals and provinces. When he returns, he and Sophie are married and settle into a life in the country. Emile is prepared for public service if it is required of him, but prefers to live in rural seclusion if he can. The book ends with Emile informing the tutor that Sophie is pregnant.

And although the purpose of his entire education has been to shape a man of integrity and confidence, he begs the tutor to help him raise his own children saying, 'Advise us and govern us. We shall be docile. As long as I live, I shall need you. I need you more than ever now that my functions as a man begin'.

RESPONSE

The critical response to *Emile* was immediate and violent, especially among people in positions of political and religious authority. Within a few weeks it was outlawed and burned in both Paris and Geneva. A warrant was issued for Rousseau's arrest in France and the Genevan authorities forbade him from returning to his native city. He was a fugitive from the law for most of the rest of his life. Some scholars have argued that these developments surprised Rousseau, yet the warnings were so many and so ominous that it is clear he knew what he was doing. Part of the explanation is that he was very ill at the time and believed himself to be dying. The cause of greatest controversy was, of course, the 'Profession of Faith of the Savoyard Vicar' along with the autobiographical narrative in which it is embedded. It was, after all, as direct and stunning an assault on organized religion as one can imagine.

One of Rousseau's most eloquent and cogent critics was the Archbishop of Paris, Christophe d'Beaumont, and Rousseau decided to respond to him with his now famous 'Letter to Beaumont', a work which offers unequalled insight into Rousseau's ideas and motivations at this time. In this masterful polemic, Rousseau simply and correctly denied the grounds for objection that Beaumont found in *Emile*. For example, he said that Beaumont should not accuse him of atheism because the 'Profession of Faith' explicitly defends the existence of God, and in any case many atheistic works were published in France without controversy. He also said that Beaumont should not accuse him of inciting civil unrest, because he explicitly argued that sovereigns have the power to control religious observance in their lands. At the same time, he offered some stunning concessions. First, he claimed that he was 'a disciple not of priests, but of Christ' which was an odd thing to say in defending himself against the Archbishop of Paris. He also confessed to denying the doctrine of original sin. And one should also add that, on Rousseau's argument, the central Christian mysteries such as the Trinity, the Eucharist and the divinity of Christ would appear to be unknowable at best, and at worst harmful superstitions.

To modern readers, however, it is not his views on religion that have been most troubling; it is rather the use he made of the concept of 'nature'. Sometimes he seems to use the terms nature and natural simply to refer to things he approved of, just as he used 'unnatural' to refer to things he disliked. This is particularly obvious in his theory of 'the natural goodness of man' and Emile's 'education according to nature'. Given that there are many cruel people just as there are many kind ones, many people who love their families and many people who hate them and so on, on what grounds can he invoke the word natural or unnatural to describe any of these phenomena? It might seem more plausible to say that it is all a matter of chance, or custom, or habit. After all, the concepts of natural and unnatural have been used to justify every kind of injustice from slavery, to discrimination, to (in Rousseau's own case) male chauvinism.

Rousseau's response was complicated but very important. Certainly he believed that human nature changes through time and that people are highly malleable to outside forces. He also agreed that the terms 'natural' and 'unnatural' have been used to justify the unjustifiable, which is the core of his argument against Aristotle's theory of natural slavery (S 43). Yet he still believed that it was possible and useful to invoke the idea of nature in psychology and moral philosophy. He said,

> Nature, we are told, is only habit. What does this mean? Are there not habits contracted only by force which never do stifle nature? Such, for example, is the habit of plants whose vertical direction is interfered with. The plant, set free, keeps the inclination it was forced to take. But the sap has not as a result changed its original direction; and if the plant continues to grow, its new growth resumes the vertical direction. The case is the same for men's inclinations. So long as one remains in the same condition, the inclinations that result from habit and are the least natural to us can be kept; but as soon as the situation changes, habit ceases and the natural returns (E 39).

The obvious objection to this line of argument is that since the environment affects all things, what they 'naturally' do cannot be separated from the environment they are in. Thus, it becomes necessary to determine which environment is the natural one, but this makes the argument circular. A thing's natural form is what it achieves in its natural environment, and its natural environment is the one that brings out its natural form. Rousseau's argument was that if the tree were 'left to itself' it would grow straight, yet if it were truly left to itself it would die for lack of sun, soil and water. The problem becomes only more profound when it returns to the question of human nature, because every child will be raised in some culture, which will contain arbitrary elements like language, manners and customs that will shape the child in one way rather than another. Thus there is a long and profound debate over whether Rousseau (and other philosophers) have succeeded in developing a moral use for the concept of 'nature'.

Another controversial aspect of his theory is the low rank he gave to the imagination. In the centuries since Rousseau's time it has become common to value children precisely for their imagination and to cultivate that faculty almost above all the others. Rousseau's educational programme weakened Emile's powers of imagination to the farthest extent possible. The reason was not that Rousseau disliked creativity. Rather he thought of imagination as precisely the power to form images, and especially images about things that one cannot understand, which he thought would create feelings and ideas that would distort a child's character. Whatever the reader's thoughts about this, Rousseau clearly saw the danger realized in his own childhood. As a young boy, he said, 'I had no idea of the facts, but I was already familiar with every feeling. I had grasped nothing; I had sensed everything', from which he traced all of his unhappiness and inefficacy. One should realize, however, that it was only because of his extraordinary power to imagine things that were not so that Rousseau could see 'the natural goodness of man' behind the wickedness of his surroundings.

A last great puzzle in *Emile* is the relationship between 'natural man' and 'civil man'. Rousseau said that it was impossible to form both at the same time, and by now it should be clear what he meant. The natural man thinks of himself as independent, while the civil man thinks of himself only as a part of a whole. At the beginning, Rousseau seemed to leave it open as to which one Emile would be. His only goal was that he should become confident, decisive, moderate and happy, and that he should be good for himself and good for others. Yet by the end he seemed to be more optimistic that the two could be joined together. Emile, it seems, is both natural and civil. He received an 'education according to nature' in which the tutor simply supplied what nature asked for and Emile ends up as an independent rural householder; yet he is also a citizen and ready to perform the duties of citizenship if they are required of him. Perhaps Rousseau was correct that 'the double object we set for ourselves could be joined in a single one by removing the contradictions of man'. This is the fundamental, unsolved question left by *Emile*, which readers must decide for themselves.

Yet the work does clarify and enrich many of Rousseau's other theories. Emile's very sophisticated education in the arts and sciences emphasizes Rousseau's point from his reply to Leszinski about the first 'Discourse', that high culture is inherently good but is often turned to evil when it is misused. It also clarifies his second 'Discourse' by showing that, in Rousseau's view, society is not inherently bad either. Emile benefits greatly by going into the wider world, including Paris, and learning his duties to others as a human being and a citizen. His social life perfects these inner qualities. The problem is not society as such, but rather the injustices of some existing societies and the way that most young people are introduced to them. Lastly, *Emile* makes it clear that Rousseau did not believe that people are inherently asocial. Part I of his second 'Discourse' does portray a state of nature in which people have no interest in each other. Yet that was a hypothetical condition, as is made clear by Emile who gradually becomes interested in love, friendship and citizenship on his own.

In any case, the influence of *Emile* on subsequent philosophers was immeasurable. It provided an educational programme based on the idea that children are not naturally evil and that they are not marked by original sin. Thus, in Rousseau's hands, education became a matter of cultivating children's inherent, natural qualities rather than beating their sinfulness out of them. This idea has echoed throughout educational theory ever since. Kant was especially struck by Rousseau's moral vision of natural simplicity and integrity. He wrote, 'I feel a consuming thirst for knowledge and a restless desire to advance in it, as well as a satisfaction in every step I take. There was a time when I thought that this alone could constitute the honor of mankind, and I despised the common man who knows nothing. Rousseau set me right. This pretended superiority vanished and I learned to respect humanity.'

CONCLUSION

Rousseau's experience on the road to Vincennes in 1749 provided him with an insight that inspired and guided all of his mature philosophical writing. He came to believe that the vices that corrupt people's characters, the injustices that pervade their social arrangements and the unhappiness from which they suffer come from human choices rather than from God or nature. The problems in society and the psychological problems of individuals are, in some sense, of their own making. He believed that people are not marked by inherent cruelty and sinfulness, and that social institutions themselves create the wickedness, violence and dissatisfaction of so much of modern life. Over the decades that followed, in diagnosing the problem and searching for cures, he built an intellectual edifice of extraordinary coherence, philosophical interest and influence.

The two most obvious influences were on the French Revolution and the Romantic movement in the arts. While in both cases the lines of influence are greatly contested, the shadow that Rousseau cast over both is indisputable. Many of the key ideas of these movements are inconceivable without his legacy, and yet both took his ideas in directions quite different from what he intended. He provided the revolutionaries with one of the most radical theories of popular sovereignty ever developed, including its declaration that all people are created equal, that rightful political power comes from the consent of the governed, that the people should make their own laws, that leaders should be accountable to the citizens and that religion is politically suspect. The revolutionaries would take these ideas to their logical extreme and beyond. Robespierre's 'Festival of the Supreme Being' in 1794 was modelled after his somewhat narrow reading of Rousseau's discussion of civil religion in *The Social*

Contract, and after Robespierre's death Rousseau's remains were transferred from Ermenonville to the Pantheon in Paris in a coffin inscribed with the words 'He demanded the rights of man'.

Rousseau himself, however, was a humanitarian rather than a revolutionary. He was more aware than anyone of the iniquities and vices of his time, but precisely because of the moral corruption that he found around him he feared revolution more than anything. He thought it was sad that people's vices were kept in check only because of a fear of punishment, yet because of these vices nothing could be worse than the breakdown of law and order. His writings diagnosed the reasons why people are unhappy and cruel and then, in his second 'Discourse' and *Emile*, he portrayed a different, better way of life, as in *The Social Contract* he depicted an idealized political organization. But nowhere did he suggest that the best route from present woes to future happiness passes through violence or revolution. On the contrary, after witnessing a revolt in Geneva he said, 'This frightful spectacle made such a strong impression on me that I vowed if ever I were to regain my rights of citizenship, never to take part in any civil war, and never to uphold domestic liberty by force of arms either in my own person or by proxy' (C 207).

To the Romantics he offered a powerful account of the goodness of nature and deep suspicion of bourgeois society, conformity and commerce. He also, perhaps unwittingly, inspired the Romantic tendency towards intense introspection. As one contemporary scholar put it, 'Modernist culture is a culture of the self par excellence. Its center is the "I" and its boundaries are defined by identity. The cult of singularity begins, as so much in modernity does, with Rousseau.' Yet it is a mistake to say, as many do, that Rousseau himself was enamoured with his own and others' emotions and sentiments. It is true that the last stage of Emile's education is the cultivation of his capacity for love and friendship, yet they are not the whole purpose of his education, which was designed instead to make him a happy individual and a useful member of society. His capacity to have intense emotions was purposely suppressed for the sake of his own happiness and that of those around him. Emile's education was designed to mollify his emotions so he could grasp the truth and live in light of it, or in light of the knowledge of his own ignorance. In his *Confessions* and *Reveries* Rousseau did give a stunning portrait of his own emotional life, but it was designed in part to show the deleterious effects of his wild emotions and over-active imagination.

Perhaps Rousseau's greatest influence, however, was on Kant and his followers, especially those who adopted Kant's general outlook but rejected his idea that the basic elements of human nature and understanding stay the same over time. On Kant's own testimony, Rousseau persuaded him of the dignity of all persons independent of rank and abilities, and Kant's theory of autonomy bears a strong similarity to the theory of 'moral freedom' developed by Rousseau in *The Social Contract*. More importantly, however, and at the risk of simplifying, one can say that Rousseau introduced historical consciousness into moral and political philosophy. Certainly he was not the first to defend the evolution of species, nor was he completely original in offering a theory of the stages of human development both in terms of the whole species and in terms of individuals. But he was one of the first, along with the Italian philosopher Giambattista Vico and the French statesman and social theorist Montesquieu, to construct a scientific social theory on the premise that people are different from place to place and time to time, and that the institutions that are best for one group might be worst for another.

This insight may seem almost trivial, yet it has profound consequences. It sets the idea of natural law on a new footing, because if human nature itself evolves then there cannot be one set of natural principles governing how a person should live. Furthermore, it leaves things open-ended at the other extreme. If people are different now from what they once were, then presumably they will be still more different in the future. While Rousseau obviously did not believe in progress in the usual sense of the word, it is very easy to find in his philosophy the roots of nineteenth-century historicism as one finds it in Marx, Nietzsche and Comte.

In this light, one can see both why so many readers have found his writings to be contradictory and also why those works, in fact, present one of the most stunningly coherent and compelling interpretations of human life and society. He appears contradictory because he approached the problems of ethics and society from the perspective of his own lived experience rather than from textbooks on morality and politics. He had almost no formal education, so he looked at things in his own way. He was influenced by his intellectual environment, of course, but the problems he took up, and the methods he used to answer them, were his own, not those that had been passed down through schools and academies. That is why he does not fit neatly into standard philosophical categories.

One cannot say which school he falls into on the key questions of the social contract, natural law, the blank slate theory of the mind, deism, perfectionism, sovereignty, commerce or the Church and state. And when he says things that cross those categories, he is thought to be incoherent. Readers expect him to take a side and to be definable as one thing rather than another. The reason that he fails this test is not that he was incoherent, but that he was original and subtle, and his concepts and methods cut across familiar categories. In the end, the contradictions that people find in his work reveal the limits of the terms in which they think about human life and society. Part of Rousseau's contribution to human self-understanding is that his works force readers to confront their own prejudices, and perhaps to see themselves for the first time.

SUGGESTIONS FOR FURTHER READING

ROUSSEAU'S LIFE AND TIMES

The best biography of Rousseau in English is Maurice Cranston's three-volume series, *Jean-Jacques: The Early Life and Work of Jean-Jacques Rousseau, 1712–1754* (Chicago, 1991), *The Noble Savage: Jean-Jacques Rousseau, 1754–1762* (Chicago, 1991) and *The Solitary Self: Jean-Jacques Rousseau in Exile and Adversity* (Chicago, 1997). For a shorter account, by a literary critic rather than a philosopher, see Leo Damrosch, *Jean-Jacques Rousseau: Restless Genius* (Boston, 2005).

For the history of France during Rousseau's lifetime, see Colin Jones, *The Great Nation: France from Louis XV to Napoleon* (London, 2002) and Daniel Roche, *France in the Enlightenment* (Cambridge, MA, 1998). The relevant history of Geneva is described in Helena Rosenblatt, *Rousseau and Geneva: From the 'First Discourse' to the 'Social Contract', 1749–1762* (Cambridge, 1997) and James Miller, *Rousseau: Dreamer of Democracy* (New Haven, 1984).

There are many excellent studies of his intellectual milieu. One may start with Dorinda Outram, *The Enlightenment* (Cambridge, 1995), and move on to such classics as Norman Hampson, *The Enlightenment* (Harmondsworth, 1968), Peter Gay's two-volume *The Enlightenment: The Rise of Modern Paganism* (New York, 1966) and *The Science of Freedom* (New York, 1969) and Ernst Cassirer, *The Philosophy of the Enlightenment* (Princeton, 1951).

ROUSSEAU'S WORKS

Rousseau's works are available in excellent editions in both French and English. The standard French edition is the five-volume *Oeuvres complètes* edited by Bernard Gagnebin and Marcel Raymond (Paris, 1959–1995). A complete edition in English is under way as *Collected Writings of Rousseau*, edited by Roger D. Masters and Christopher Kelly (Hanover, NH, 1990–). His letters have been published in 52 volumes as *Correspondance complète de Jean-Jacques Rousseau*, edited by R. A. Leigh (Geneva, 1965–1998).

There are exemplary translations of Rousseau's major political writings by Victor Gourevitch in *The Discourses and Other Early Political Writings* and *The Social Contract and Other Later Political Writings* (Cambridge, 1997). Allan Bloom made an excellent translation of *Emile; or On Education* (New York, 1979).

INTERPRETATIONS OF ROUSSEAU'S PHILOSOPHY

For accessible introductions to Rousseau's thought see Nicholas Dent, *Rousseau* (London, 2005), Robert Wokler, *Rousseau: A Very Short Introduction* (Oxford, 2001) and Timothy O'Hagan, *Rousseau* (London, 1999).

The most interesting attempts to find the overall meaning of Rousseau's philosophy include David Gauthier, *Rousseau: The Sentiment of Existence* (Cambridge, 2006), Tzvetan Todorov, *Frail Happiness: An Essay on Rousseau* (University Park, 2001), Arthur M. Melzer, *The Natural Goodness of Man: On the System of Rousseau's Thought* (Chicago, 1990), Jean Starobinski, *Jean-Jacques Rousseau: Transparency and Obstruction* (Chicago, 1988), Ronald Grimsley, *The Philosophy of Rousseau* (Oxford, 1973) and Ernst Cassirer, *The Question of Jean-Jacques Rousseau* (New York, 1963). Readers might also benefit from the essays in Patrick Riley (ed.), *The Cambridge Companion to Rousseau* (Cambridge, 2001).

For Rousseau's political thought in particular, among the best overviews are Maurizio Viroli, *Jean-Jacques Rousseau and the 'Well-Ordered Society'* (Cambridge, 1988), Judith Shklar, *Men and Citizens: A Study of Rousseau's Social Theory* (Cambridge, 1985), John Charvet, *The Social Problem in the Philosophy of Jean-Jacques Rousseau* (Cambridge, 1974) and Roger D. Masters, *The Political Philosophy of Rousseau* (Princeton, 1968).

The books listed above offer excellent discussions of Rousseau's individual works, but readers will also profit from more specialized treatments. For his 'Discourse on the Sciences and Arts' see Victor Gourevitch, 'Rousseau on the Arts and Sciences', *Journal of Philosophy*, vol. 69, no. 20 (1972). For his 'Discourse on the Origin of Inequality', see the famous essay by Arthur O. Lovejoy, 'Rousseau's Supposed Primitivism', in his *Essays in the History of Ideas* (Baltimore, 1948). For a contextual analysis of both 'Discourses' see Mario Einaudi, *The Early Rousseau* (Ithaca, 1967).

Regarding *The Social Contract*, see Christopher Bertram, *The Routledge Philosophy Guidebook to Rousseau and the Social Contract* (London, 2004) and Hilail Gildin, *Rousseau's Social Contract: The Design of the Argument* (Chicago, 1983). For *Emile*, see Allan Bloom's introduction to his translation of that work, listed above. The philosophical dimensions of Rousseau's autobiographies are discussed in Christopher Kelly, *Rousseau's Exemplary Life: The Confessions as Political Philosophy* (Ithaca, 1987). And for the philosophical importance of Rousseau's last work, *Reveries of a Solitary Walker*, see Eli Friedlander, *Jean-Jacques Rousseau: An Afterlife in Words* (Cambridge, MA, 2004).

For the controversial and interesting question of Rousseau's views on gender, see Elizabeth Rose Wingrove, *Rousseau's Republican Romance* (Princeton, 2000), Joel Schwartz, *The Sexual Politics of Jean-Jacques Rousseau* (Chicago, 1985) and the chapter on Rousseau in Susan Moller Okin, *Women in Western Political Thought* (Princeton, 1979).

INFLUENCE AND LEGACY

For Rousseau's effect on the philosophers of his time see Graeme Garrard, *Rousseau's Counter-Enlightenment: A Republican Critique of the Philosophes* (Albany, 2003) and Mark Hulliung, *The Autocritique of the Enlightenment: Rousseau and the Philosophes* (Cambridge, MA, 1994).

Rousseau's influence on the French Revolution is discussed in Carol Blum, *Rousseau and the Republic of Virtue: The Language of Politics in the French Revolution* (Ithaca, 1986). For his influence on Romanticism see Thomas MacFarland, *Romanticism and the Heritage of Rousseau* (Oxford, 1995) and Irving Babbitt's famous critique, *Rousseau and Romanticism* (Boston, 1919). For a general survey of his influence, see Clifford Orwin and Nathan Tarcov (eds), *The Legacy of Rousseau* (Chicago, 1997).

INDEX